Rehabilitation of Offenders and Role of Counselling

REHABILITATION OF OFFENDERS AND ROLE OF COUNSELLING

Editor

J. C. Chaturvedi

ISHA

ISHA BOOKS

DELHI-110033

Rehabilitation of Offenders and Role of Counselling

Rs. 750

ISBN: 81-8205-352-8

Published in 2006 in India by
Isha Books
D-43, Prithviraj Road,
Adarsh Nagar, Delhi-110033
e-mail : ishabooks@hotmail.com

Laser Typesetting at : Shiva Infosystem, Delhi
Printed at : Mehra Offset Press, Delhi

Preface

A wide range of rehabilitation services are available to aid recovery and rehabilitation of people suffering from serious mental health problems. New Patterns of Obsession and Trauma provides new perspectives on the prevalence, causes, and effects of stalking in intimate and non-intimate relations. Drawing on the results of a large random survey of restraining orders, this book found that stalking is highly prevalent in a variety of relationships and is a pattern of behaviours that is routinely regulated by the demographic and social characteristics of the victims and offenders. This book demonstrates that it is possible to develop reliable stalker profiles to help better detect and respond to the threat of stalking.

Covering a wide range of topics from offender profiling, the dangers of stalking, cyberstalking, traumatic health effects, and the responses of the police and courts to stalking, this book will be relevant to a wide range of professionals and students in the fields of mental health, criminal justice, law, social work, medicine, nursing, public health, security/safety, and internet technology.

Editor

Contents

1

Criminal Justice Interventions

Criminalisation seeks to introduce the standards and norms of non-violence in public places, and the means of enforcing and regulating these, into people's more intimate lives. Criminalisation attempts to insert the power and authority of 'the state' between a person prepared to use physical force and/or the threat of it, and the persons over whom such dominion and control is sought.

Demands for criminalisation of domestic violence found fertile ground, over the past three decades, in wider struggles for gender equity, the 'rights' of crime victims, and in political pressure for crime control and 'law and order'. However, the criminal justice system's response to domestic violence has been, and continues to be, the subject of extensive and persisting criticism by researchers and victim advocates.

Notwithstanding efforts such as these, some advocates and researchers in the domestic and family violence field have begun to raise questions about criminalisation, its unintended consequences, and its primacy over other forms of intervention and prevention. These questions raise many challenges and dilemmas for researchers, survivor advocates and criminal justice organisations.

This chapter explores some of the contemporary debates and dilemmas in implementing criminal justice reform in the area of domestic violence. This exploration is based on presentation and discussion of key research findings. In doing so it does not claim that criminal justice should be the sole or even primary strategy employed to tackle domestic violence.

On the contrary, given that so few victims of domestic violence actually seek criminal justice intervention, it could be argued that criminal justice should be a minor player alongside community-based and primary health reforms. However, criminal justice performs a function that is not only instrumental in enforcing legal and social norms, but is highly symbolic. Criminal law is a powerful agency of public disapproval and reprobation.

The criminal justice system purports to deliver under the banner-waving terms of justice, upholding citizens' rights, and protecting the vulnerable. For victims of domestic violence and their advocates, criminal justice interventions are one means of society delivering concrete meaning on these terms. It is also provides one of the few mechanisms available to victims for actually stopping the violence.

In so doing it focuses on police, prosecution, criminal courts, and community corrections - agencies of the criminal justice system. It assumes some level of knowledge of those agencies and of some basic legal concepts which underpin criminal jurisprudence. It does not examine legislative reform, and access and procedural issues with regard to the granting of protection orders. The enforcement of protection orders is addressed only as a function of the broader obligation of law enforcement agencies to investigate allegations of criminal conduct.

Responses to perpetrators of domestic violence are addressed in a relatively limited fashion as being the range of options before the court pre and post hearing, and as issues for probation and parole in managing offenders. Some of the key research into perpetrator programs - whether courtmandated or 'voluntary' or some mix in between -has already been extensively covered. It should be noted, however, that research in this area is evolving rapidly and will be the subject of a future issues paper from the Clearinghouse. The consequent reliance on overseas research, and the limitations and potential traps which arise, are outlined.

This chapter turns from the exploration of informal supports, to the world of formal criminal justice interventions. It is claimed that the foundations of a fair system of justice in Australia are openness and accountability at all stages, fairness and balance, expedition, efficiency and cost effectiveness. Australia's criminal justice agencies are expected to deliver on these lofty aims as they confront fiscal realities familiar to other public services.

Key material and political pressures facing decisionmakers and administrators include efficiency, timeliness, managing the volume of cases, cost of justice, legal aid cuts, effectiveness, accountability, meeting community expectations, alternative dispute resolution, and technological advances. Reforms in the domestic violence area must acknowledge and take place in this wider context.

Those advocating reform in the criminal justice response to domestic violence also need to acknowledge sometimes competing expectations and pressures on, and perceptions and experiences of, criminal justice itself. Many social justice commentators, for example, have expressed concern about responses that effectively criminalise social and behavioural problems such as substance misuse or juvenile delinquency.

Others have pointed out the disproportionate impact of criminal justice interventions on sections of the population such as homeless people, and the experience by Indigenous communities of law enforcement as agents of colonisation and discrimination. In this context, feminists have sometimes been drawn into unlikely and uncomfortable alliances with 'law and order' advocates for more police, tougher judges and harsher sentences.

Criminal justice is a blunt-edged instrument in complex social and inter-personal issues. Its cumbersome machinery is reactive rather than proactive. It is incident-based, patriarchal, hierarchical, defendant-focussed, and generally not research driven in its interventions. Reformers have sometimes placed a lot of energy and expectation on one-off solutions or quick fixes. Debates about whether the criminal justice system is there for deterrence, rehabilitation, retribution, or restoration, also lap the edges of domestic violence reforms.

Role of the Victim within the Criminal Justice System

Todays criminal justice system utilises 'the State' as surrogate victim and the real crime victim is relegated to a role of lead witness. For most victims of crime, domestic violence included, even their role as lead witness never comes as so few incidents enter the criminal justice system by way of reports to police. For the most part, until recently, crime victims had no rights at all, 'only courtesies to be extended or withheld at the whim of the police or prosecutor.'

In part to address this situation, legislative, service and procedural reforms aimed at addressing crime victims' concerns about the criminal justice system have been introduced in most Western jurisdictions. To a large extent, these reforms have resulted from campaigning by crime victim groups and their supporters. However, because the histories and activities of the movement against violence against women and that advancing the interests of victims of other crime have been relatively separate, knowledge, understanding and use of these codes has been limited to date in domestic violence reforms.

In essence these codes provide a framework for the crime victim to be incorporated in the procedures and key decisionmaking points of criminal processing and confer obligations on criminal justice agencies that are both concrete and measurable, thereby enhancing transparency and accountability. In some jurisdictions, this includes a means of independently monitoring and reporting on performance and effectiveness.

These reforms have been met with caution and even resistance by practitioners and administrators within the system. Studies show that within the judicial branch, prosecutors, defence lawyers, and judges operate as a 'work group', sharing the mutual goal of disposing of cases as fast as time and justice will allow. This work group feared victim reforms would slow down or derail functional efficiency.

Even amongst victim advocates and researchers, there is fierce debate about the role of the crime victim in the criminal justice system; about the capacity, willingness and effectiveness of the system to deliver key victim needs; and the impact of participating in the system on victims themselves and on justice agencies.

Current areas of discuss and evaluation acknowledge that, even in jurisdictions which have legislated for crime victims' rights, it is still by luck and good fortune rather than good government and effective client service that crime victims as a 'class' in society receive these rights in a consistent and comprehensive fashion.

Critiques of Criminal Justice

Women's participation in the criminal justice system as victims of domestic violence comes about with or without choice. Like most people, crime victims do not necessarily know anything about the various functions of its agencies, its procedures and standards of proof, and the victim/witness role within it. Some may say that it is ironic that feminists elicit state intervention in women's interests from agencies that represent the pinnacle of patriarchal power. Yet the fear that stalks many women living with domestic violence means that, more often than not, the protection ostensibly offered by police is critically necessary, if often faulty in execution.

When a woman being beaten by her partner calls the emergency police number she dials into a complex system, which usually resolves cases based on institutional imperatives rather than on making victim safety central. Yet for nearly 20 years the justice system has consumed much of the energy of the various movements against domestic violence:

The judicial system was criticized for failure to act independently of the victim against the use of violence and for its inability to protect the victim during the court process. Insistence by the police and prosecutors that women initiate and pursue legal action against abusers ignored the realities of battering and rendered the courts useless to most victims of battering. When promoting legal reform, it is essential to understand the different roles and functions of the various criminal justice agencies. For those already engaged in improving coordinated responses, it becomes critically important to learn about the powers and levers that each agency has or potentially has in processing a domestic violence case.

Audit is one means whereby practitioners within the system can review this micro-processing of cases with a view to reform. The criticisms of the criminal justice system's response to domestic violence have been extensively documented. It is, however, worthwhile re-capping some of them. The range of dilemmas and concerns have included:

— criminal justice agencies traditionally did not treat family and especially domestic violence matters seriously,

— despite a policy position that domestic violence is a crime, low charge and conviction rates suggested it was being otherwise considered,

— there is a lack of systemic and case coordination within and across criminal justice agencies,

— neither victim safety nor perpetrator accountability are practically and consistently addressed by criminal justice agencies,

— insufficient attention was being paid to 'belief on reasonable grounds', evidence gathering, victim safety and arrest options at the time of the incident,

— there appear to be irreconcilable dilemmas in balancing victim ambivalence over whether to proceed with responsibilities to uphold the criminal law and protect vulnerable persons.

— domestic violence matters 'dropped' too easily from the prosecution process,

— difficulties in proceeding with ambivalent or hostile witnesses,

— difficulties in matching victim services to victim needs at the 'right' time,

— a lack of procedural fairness for victims including timely notifications,

— options for victim participation in the process were non-existent,

— length of time for criminal domestic violence matters to be heard in court and court delays that create further 'attrition' on the victim,

— sentencing options are ineffective in reducing repeat offending, do not provide for victim input, and pay insufficient attention to compliance with court orders,

— ineffective or non-existent mechanisms for gaining victim information as to the history and context of the abuse for police, prosecutors, courts and corrections.

In response to these critiques, justice agencies have responded in a variety of ways. Some initiatives include specialisms in police action at domestic violence incidents such as the NDV pilot project in South Australia, assertive prosecution practices and the availability of witness assistance within prosecution (ACT), specialised courts, probation responses and offender management issues, and closer working relationships between criminal justice agencies and domestic violence support/advocacy staff.

Victim Decision-making in Legal Interventions

The responses of justice agencies to victims of domestic violence focussed on under-enforcement and under-utilisation of laws, chronic victim-blaming, inconsistency, and inadequate or inappropriate responses. Together, these studies noted the general failure of the legal system to provide options or respond in ways that were meaningful, effective or positive for the victim. More recently, attention has focussed on the actions taken by victims themselves, commonly called helpseeking state that 'virtually everyone has some experience in helpseeking, from medical care to lawn services to caterers or therapists'. As a social behaviour, there is nothing unusual about help-seeking efforts. In contrast, 'survivor theory' suggests that abused women are very active in measures that seek to 'manage', cope with and/or extricate themselves from the violence. Furthermore, they will make greater efforts to protect themselves and their children by increasing their help-seeking as abuse increases.

Feminist criminologists such as Dr Elizabeth Stanko and Professor Jane Ursel consequently now argue for a re-thinking of the criminal justice system as a 'resource not a solution' in women's struggles to end violence in their lives. In essence, help-seeking and the responses it brings is part of a continual daily weighing up process for women facing abusive behaviours in their lives. Decisions made and paths taken one day may be derailed by an unsupportive and victim-blaming response, or overturned by an incident of severe violence the next day.

A range of factors have been shown to impact on a victim's decision to seek help from the police - the gatekeepers to the criminal justice system. For example, some found that the length of the abusive relationship impacted on general help-seeking, and that continued helpseeking was affected by the response received and the impact of that response on the abusive behaviour. Factors identified as inclining a victim towards calling the police include assault severity, husband's unemployment, wife's unemployment, and alcohol use; situational variables such as prior history of calling police; severity and frequency of abuse, dependent children, length of time in the abusive relationship, and alcohol use by the abuser.

People who were married were found to be consistently more oriented to obtaining help about domestic violence from a range of social and legal sources than were cohabitants. However, victims who cohabit do use police more readily than do victims who are married. Two US experiments found that women from different racial groups seek the same amount of assistance but that white Americans are more likely to use social services and African-Americans to call the police or a minister. These findings are consistent with figures produced by the Metropolitan Police (UK) for the Hammersmith and Fulham Domestic Violence Forum in the early 1990s showing that African-Caribbean women called for police assistance in numbers slightly higher than their proportion of the population. However, Neville and Pugh's exploration of African American women reporting sexual assault did find that a general distrust of police was a significant inhibitor.

Criminal Justice System

Having once initiated legal intervention through a call for police assistance, the situation then becomes ever more complex for the victim and justice personnel. A consistent frustration heard from police and prosecutors concerns their perception of women's readiness to seek to have a matter dropped or withdrawn following police intervention. They often interpret women's help-seeking from them as ambivalent at best or capricious at worst. Some found out that, in the majority of domestic incidents to which police responded, it was not the intention of the victim to have the perpetrator arrested. Furthermore, when an arrest did occur, the majority of victims did not wish to proceed with prosecution.

On this critical issue, US studies have documented the frequency with which some victims of domestic violence seek to drop criminal charges and have noted that this frequency is significantly greater than in other kinds of criminal cases. Unfortunately this calculations did not examine whether the use of prosecution witness assistants or external advocates impacted on the level of victim 'cooperation'. In response, women's advocates have drawn attention to the need for practitioners to understand the dynamics of violence, the 'cycle of violence', and the impact of violence. Australia's only research into this issue comes from the ACT's Family Violence Intervention Program. Of those victims whose matter had been finalised, 51 per cent were "determined to see the case through no matter what" whilst 26 per cent had indicated at some point that they had wanted the charges dropped. This evaluation goes on to illuminate the link between a victim's views about the prosecution proceeding and victim satisfaction with prosecution authorities.

Some experiments describe women's fear and sense of powerlessness and helplessness in picking a tortuous way through the paths of criminal, civil and family law, social and community assistance, and informal support. Others emphasise women's 'strategic management' of the violence and the help-giving resources available to her. Women consistently describe fear of retaliation as impacting on decisions to seek withdrawal from the criminal justice process. This is born out by their actual experience of repeat assaults following police and court intervention.

Some found that women with a substance abuse problem were only half as likely as other women to follow through with prosecution. Other factors such as depression or attachment to the abuser were not found to be predictive of follow-through. Perhaps most importantly, their study found that women with tangible material and social support from family and friends were twice as likely to follow through as those without.

Some experiments of a model prosecution jurisdiction in Indiana suggest that victims who come into the system are not helpless or passive but, rather, actively use a strategy to get what they need. They often seek to leave the system when they achieve - in the short or longer term - what they have sought to do. Hence, Ford suggests that women utilise the criminal justice system as a 'power resource'.

In their English study, Hoyle and Sanders concur and further suggest that women's 'decisions are rationally chosen in the context of their current lives [and that] women are, therefore, situationally coerced by their circumstances' given that 'their choices are formed within relationships where controlling behaviours are prevalent'.

In the first instance, victims described how confusing the system and the process was to them. Secondly, they described a depth of frustration with the system's slowness and the range cf what they experienced as bureaucratic barriers. Thirdly, women described the time between the batterer's arrest and the resolution of the court case as being one of 'paralysing fear'.

Finally, many women felt considerable internal conflict over the prospect of punitive sanctions such as incarceration. The large African-American sample in these studies point to this community's experience of a discriminatory and oppressive criminal justice system. Many women also expressed a wish that the perpetrator 'gets help' and felt conflict over his relationship with shared children, a finding common to other research. In understanding these sometimes practical impediments, the researchers argue that 'the task we can approach is that of reshaping or fine tuning the system [women] encounter'.

Some of the feminist, therapeutic and jurisprudential implications of these issues are explored in excellent articles by Cheryl Hanna and Linda Mills. Whereas the previous studies describe women's decision-making and women's experience in the system, these articles consider the implications for professional decision-making on whether or not to proceed with prosecution. Hanna explores the dilemmas faced as a prosecutor in whether or not to compel a reluctant or hostile domestic violence victim/witness. She employs the term mandated participation in preference to that of victim cooperation in balancing her desire for a public response to the violence and preserving women's autonomy from excessive state intervention. Hanna concludes that there can never be an adequate resolution to the 'victim/agent dichotomy in the criminal context' or indeed the 'particularity/ generality' tension in feminism itself.

Mills and others further condemn taking the choice away from the victim as it is therapeutically damaging, socially disempowering and leaves her in danger. Ruttenberg and Fedders go further to strongly criticise the current US emphasis for a compelling and criminalising response as critically detrimental to women of colour and poor women. Having better knowledge of the complex motives for help-seeking of abused women, who they seek help from, and in what circumstances, is critical to understanding their interaction with legal institutions and the context in which it occurs.

Police Response to Domestic Violence

In an emergency, police are the most likely agency to be called for assistance. Their actions are critically important. In brief, criticisms of police practice have included that police do not respond to domestic violence as a serious crime problem; that the assistance they do or do not provide both victim and perpetrator is ineffective and unsuitable; that they have ignored the needs of child witnesses to violence; that the attention paid to investigation and evidence collection has been negligible; that domestic violence cases were routinely and ruthlessly screened out; and that police management has consistently ignored these failures and not provided sufficient training, monitoring, supervision or policy and practice guidance. Prior to the US arrest studies, there was a common presumption that there was little police could do about domestic violence. One of the earliest known US studies, however, found that domestic violence was repetitive and highly visible to police.

As previously stated, the predominant policy claim in Australia, New Zealand, the USA, Canada and the UK is that domestic violence is a crime. Whilst all behaviours common in domestic violence relationships may not constitute criminal offences, nonetheless law enforcement agencies in these countries have instituted policies that promote arrest and charge as a primary intervention where there is a 'belief on reasonable grounds' that an offence may have been committed. The range of reasons for this include:

- Arrest is the only response that can guarantee the immediate cessation of violence and the short term protection of the victim
- It upholds law enforcement as a primary police role, a role that only police have
- It limits discretionary action based on the influence of attitudinal variables that bear no relation to forming a 'belief on reasonable grounds'
- Arrest acts to provide a gateway for both victims and perpetrators to a range of services
- It acts as an individual and public deterrent to further offending
- It sends a message to the community that the use of violence within relationships and families is unacceptable
- In the USA, civil actions against police departments on negligent failure to act have cost millions of dollars in damages

— Finally, some evidence exists that, for some offenders in some circumstances, arrest alone can prevent re-offending

Family Violence Reports to Police

Studies differ on the level of reporting of domestic violence to police as a proportion of the total number of incidents. The range is from two per cent to 50 per cent. In Australia, the National Women's Safety Survey identified that, of women who had experienced violence, 20 per cent called for police assistance. This latter figure is consistent with other national surveys in Canada and New Zealand.

The primary coercive sanction available to police is an arrest. However, they also have a range of other legally sanctioned options such as removal of an intoxicated person into protective custody, and removing a vulnerable person into authorised or secure premises. Whilst arrest is a crude measure of police performance in any offence category, the disinclination to arrest in family violence incidents has been noted in Australia and other countries. These studies reveal an arrest rate varying from 3 per cent to 13.9 per cent. However, Feder found that the likelihood of arrest in domestic violence incidents was double that for non-domestic assault incidents.

In the ACT, Mugford, Easteal and Edwards identified that, over a three month period in 1991, six per cent of domestic violence incidents resulted in an arrest and charge. The current ACT Family Violence Intervention Program (FVIP) identified that 'positive action' was taken in 47 per cent of all incidents (of 297 incidents) attended by Woden Patrol over nine months in 2000-2001. Arrest constitutes 27 per cent of all domestic incidents. These findings suggest that policy makers and researchers need to look more closely at the content of incidents in order to determine the appropriateness or otherwise of police action.

Variables in Arrest Decision

The decision to arrest in any given circumstance has been shown to be made with regard to a wide range of variables. The variables include demographic characteristics of victims and offenders (e.g. race, marital status), demographic characteristics of police officers (e.g. gender, length of experience), attitudinal variables (e.g. victim preference for arrest and officers' attitudes), and situational variables, such as whether a weapon is involved.

There is continuing debate in the literature about the victim's preference for or against arrest following police intervention. In part this results from research design. Mostly, however, studies do not adequately draw out how this preference is influenced by different factors at different times of the victim's life vis a vis the violent relationship. Often the issue about 'preference' is conflated with victim 'cooperativeness'.

The data on attitudinal variables illustrate the complexity of the construct of victim 'cooperativeness'. A common finding is that the victim's preference for arrest significantly increases the likelihood of arrest at the scene. However, the victim's preferences are more likely to be followed if officers considered the victims to be rational and respectful rather than verbally abusive or intoxicated, or they believed she had not invited the perpetrator into the home.

When officers believed that the victim was 'uncooperative' or would seek to have charges dropped, they were less likely to make arrests. Officers' belief in the likelihood of prosecution and victim participation in that process significantly increased the officers' perception of the victim as 'cooperative'. Officers' rating of victim 'cooperativeness' significantly decreased when the officer believed the victim had a probable drug or alcohol problem, when alcohol or drugs were present at the scene, and the longer the tenure of the officer. Interestingly, when an arrest was not made at the scene, victims were significantly less likely to participate in the prosecution of their cases.

It is pleasing to note that situational or legal variables are found to be more important predictors of the arrest decision than are extra-legal variables such as attitude or demographics. Some of these are when a weapon is involved, that weapon being a gun or sharp object rather than a blunt object or bodily weapon; seriousness of the offence; additional witnesses and children present; evidence of forced entry; incidents of repeat violence and signs of struggle.

The presence of the suspect at the scene is the most powerful of the situational variables. It is also possible that the factors listed as variables in the decision to arrest may not be predictors but may in fact be occurring simultaneously. There is a real gap in linking research into the organisational features known to shape how officers work, and their activities in relation to domestic violence.

Some of the former variables that could be examined as influential include levels of supervision, the ways in which activities are structured, reward systems, the disparity between formal rules and informal practice, local patterns in non-domestic crime, local political and community priorities, and the climate of policing in particular locations. Interestingly, some studies point to the importance to police of coordinated criminal justice interventions.

Effect of Arrest

The Minneapolis Arrest Experiment has had a powerful effect on law enforcement and policy makers around the world. This experiment was initiated under the National Institute of Justice Crime Control Theory Program to test the theory of specific deterrence and in response to calls for more rigorous research methodology. The experiment found that arrest was more predicative of a reduction in repeat violence than giving advice or removing the alleged perpetrator from the scene. The US National Institute of Justice concluded that these experiments suggest arrest is an effective option in reducing repeat violence in the short term and with perpetrators who are not on low incomes and who are employed.

Some initiatives in Australia have moved beyond the 'arrest or not arrest' debate to examine ways of improving investigative practice and brief preparation in domestic violence cases. These initiatives emphasise evidence-gathering as a critical police function that has maximum impact on agencies further up the line in the criminal justice system, that is, prosecution, courts and corrections. In areas in both NSW and Queensland, for example, police are experimenting with the use of Polaroid cameras as evidence gathering tools.

The ACT's coordinated criminal justice initiative, the Family Violence Intervention Program (FVIP), also emphasises improved investigative practice imbedded within a project comprising detailed training, close management and monitoring, new technology, and closer working relationships between the Office of the DPP and the non-government Domestic Violence Crisis Service (DVCS).

In the evaluation of Phase II of the FVIP, 64-69 per cent of officers in the pilot patrol of Woden believe that the quality of their investigative practice and evidence gathering, briefs of evidence have improved since the introduction of new training and new technology. The impact of this emphasis on skilling and equipping officers as professionals in evidence gathering has had significant results. The arrest rate of all incidents in the pilot patrol area has increased from 16 per cent to 27 per cent. In Phase I of the FVIP about 70 per cent of criminal family violence matters proceeded to full hearing. In Phase II, this has almost reversed with 60-70 per cent of defendants entering a guilty plea at the mention stage.

This saves the victim from the stress of waiting time and appearance at court. It also entails direct cost saving to the police and court. Prosecutors attribute these results in part to the better quality of evidence prepared by police. Certainly, the closer liaison between the Office of the DPP and police in the ACT on evidence and brief preparation has been an important innovation.

Prosecution Intervention

The responses to domestic violence of prosecution authorities in Australia has been minimally examined by policy-makers and advocates, and is severely under-researched. Perhaps this can be attributed to the fact that the role and activities of prosecution have been less in the public spotlight and far less accessible to activists and researchers than have law enforcement agencies.

The preponderance of criminal cases involving domestic violence, and certainly the majority of those involving lesser injuries, are prosecuted in Australia by police prosecutors. The existence of independent Directors of Public Prosecutions is a relatively recent innovation. Research into both types of prosecution authorities is negligible in Australia.

The role of prosecution is classically misunderstood by victims of crime and those working with them. The prosecutor represents the state or the community, and is not a lawyer or advocate for the crime victim. In the US, women's and legal activists and the Violence Against Women Act 1994 have consolidated this role in domestic violence justice reform. US prosecutors have moved from a being criticised as 'the weak link' in the criminal justice system, to being lauded as being 'in a unique position to influence' it. As mentioned previously, the perception and reality of the prosecutor's actions and decisions are key influences over police decision-making. They can also be strongly influential in court decision-making.

Nonetheless, prosecutors can claim with some justification that the issue with low prosecution and conviction rates is precisely that related to victim cooperation. In many domestic violence cases, victim testimony is the main, if not only, source of evidence. For this to be retracted or denied can be fatal to the prosecution case. Prosecutors therefore have tended to err on the side of caution and to screen such cases out before they are tested at court.

A range of innovations in the prosecution of domestic violence are being tested in North America and Australia both in response to the criticisms noted above, and in part because of pressures on the system as a whole to become more efficient and more outcome focussed. Some of these innovations include: the implementation of assertive prosecution policies and practices; establishing specialist prosecution positions or units; the use of victim support/ witness assistance; closer liaison with police on evidence gathering, brief preparation and training; and creating links with corrections for improved monitoring of offender compliance with court orders.

2

Criminal Harassment

Criminal harassment is an offence in the Criminal Code. It is harassing behaviour that includes stalking. The behaviour must give you good reason to fear for your personal safety and it must have no legitimate purpose. Generally, the behaviour must happen not just once but repeatedly. However, where the behaviour is overtly threatening, a single incident may be considered criminal harassment. It is not an excuse for the person to claim that he or she did not intend to frighten you.

Remember, though, some people do have a lawful reason to contact you repeatedly. For example, a debt collector may call you several times. Although you may not like this contact, it is lawful when done according to laws regulating collections. Here are some examples of criminal harassment:

- calling you over and over again, and perhaps hanging up whenever you answer the phone
- contacting you on the Internet or through constant e-mail messages
- following you, your family or friends
- leaving threatening voice messages

— sending you gifts you do not want

— watching you or tracking where you go

— threatening you, your children, family, pets or friends

These are common examples. Such unwanted behaviour can be frightening and cause emotional distress. You can take action if this is happening to you. Contact the police to discuss your options.

Harassment and stalking have been around for a long time, but the specific Criminal Code offence of "criminal harassment" was only created in 1993. In the past, the police would charge a person with an offence like trespassing at night, loitering or uttering threats. These crimes still exist and may still be charged. However, since 1993 the police usually address this type of conduct through a charge of criminal harassment.

Stalkers have a variety of personalities and characteristics. Some may have a mental disorder. Experts have described many types of stalkers, but they mostly fit into two basic categories:

— *Stalkers obsessed with a stranger* : fixate on a stranger, sometimes a celebrity. They may believe their conduct will eventually win the love of their victim. Or they may have delusions that the victim already loves them but cannot return their affection because of some external influence. In Canada, about 12% of victims of criminal harassment are harassed by a stranger.

— *Stalkers obsessed with someone they know*: Many stalkers know their victims and are trying to control them, whether they are ex-partners, spouses, acquaintances, co-workers or close friends. About 88% of criminal harassment victims fall into this category. In many cases, the stalking is an extension of family violence.

It is hard to know if the person harassing you will become violent. You should ask the police to help you assess the risk. Less than 1% of criminal harassment cases involve injury to the victim. However, when criminal harassment is a continuation of a family violence situation the risk of violence is greater. It is always a good idea to find ways to increase your safety.

Being harassed or stalked is not your fault. The person may claim to love you, but he or she really wants to control you. You have the right to reject a friendship, separate from a spouse, or break up with a partner. Just because you know the person does not mean that you must put up with the harassing behaviour. You are not to blame if someone repeatedly bothers you or follows you around. Remember, what they are doing is NOT love. It is against the law and you can take action.

Taking Action

What can do if someone is stalking or harassing me?

— Think about your safety and get help. The first thing to do is call the police.

— Dial 911 if you are in immediate danger.

— Call the regular police number to discuss other criminal harassment offences.

— Tell the police what is happening.

— Let the police know that you fear for your safety or for the safety of someone you know.

— Ask for support and information to help you cope.

Your safety is important to the police. The police can suggest ways to stop unwanted contact and improve your safety. They can put you in touch with others who can help. This might include victim service workers, transition houses, or crisis and counselling services. They may also suggest safety measures such as getting an unlisted phone number.

The police will investigate the complaint. They will ask about the harassment and collect as much evidence as possible. They may take photographs of damaged property and ask for any written records. The officer will write a report about the incident and ask you to prepare a written statement of your complaint.

The police need as much evidence as possible, so try to keep the following:

— Any relevant details that you know about the person. For example, does he or she have a gun, a criminal record, or an existing court order not to contact you?

— Written records with details about every contact.

— These records will help if you go to court. Ask your friends to keep records too if the person is contacting them.

— Things the person sent you, such as notes, gifts, or phone messages.

— A list of witnesses, including names and telephone numbers.

If there is enough evidence of an offence, the police will charge the person. In some provinces, the police must consult with the Crown prosecutor before they lay charges. However, if the police do not charge the person, it does not mean that they do not believe you.

There may not be enough evidence to support a charge and the police may suggest other legal options such as a peace bond, restraining order or protection order.

Depending on what has happened and the type of evidence, the police might charge the person with one or more Criminal Code offences, such as:

- criminal harassment
- trespassing at night
- assault
- uttering threats
- intimidation

Will the person harassing me be arrested and sent to jail? The answer is not simple. It depends on the facts and the seriousness of the behaviour. The police will assess each situation and take the appropriate action under the circumstances. For example, if the police do not arrest the person, they may require him or her to sign a "promise to appear" in court to answer the charge. Tell the police and victim services if you still fear for your safety. If the police do make an arrest, ask them to let you know if they release the person from custody. If the person goes before a judge or a Justice of the Peace, which usually happens within hours, he or she might be:

- released on an "undertaking" (a promise that usually has conditions to stay away from the victim and other related persons);
- released on bail after signing a "recognizance" (a promise to appear in court which includes a financial penalty for not showing up and perhaps restrictions like promising not to contact you); or
- kept in jail until the trial. This might happen if the crime was serious and the court believes the person may not show up, or will commit another offence before the trial.

If charges are laid, the police will turn the file over to the Crown prosecutor's office. The Crown prosecutor is responsible for taking the case to court. If the accused person pleads guilty, you may not have to go to court. If he or she pleads not guilty, the Crown prosecutor would summon you as a witness at the trial to prove that the person committed the crime. Ask for help from victim services. A victim service worker can answer questions about what will happen in court, and keep you updated on the status of your case. They can also make sure you have an interpreter in court if you need one. You can contact the Crown prosecutor in your case if you have questions about the evidence you will present in court.

What happens if the person is found guilty? If the accused person pleads guilty or is found guilty, the judge will decide the sentence. Before sentencing, you can give the court a written victim impact statement describing how the crime affected you. If you wish, you may read the statement at the sentencing hearing. The sentence for a criminal harassment conviction may range from jail in the most serious cases (up to 10 years) to probation in less serious cases. Probation orders can include conditions such as no contact. The court can also impose a fine. The exact sentence depends on many factors - whether violence was used, whether the person already has a criminal record, whether drugs and alcohol were involved, and so on.

Legal Options

— This is a court order under the Criminal Code made by a provincial court judge, or an agreement the person makes with the court, for a period up to 12 months.

— It can include reasonable conditions such as not to visit you, not to contact you, your children or family, not to have guns, and so on.

— You may wish to consider a peace bond if you have good reason to feel that someone like an ex-partner will harm you, your children or property.

— To request a peace bond, go to the nearest police station. You may need a lawyer. In some provinces a Crown prosecutor or victim services will make the application for you. A peace bond may take several weeks to get, and it applies only in the province that issued it.

— If the person breaks any conditions, call the police immediately. This person may be charged for breaking conditions, and if convicted, he or she could be sent to jail or fined, or both, and would also get a criminal record.

Restraining order

— A restraining order is not a criminal order. It is a family court order made under provincial civil law. It forbids a spouse or partner from molesting, annoying, harassing you or communicating with you and the children, except as set out in the order.

— It serves basically the same function as a peace bond but does not necessarily carry the same penalties if the person disobeys it. To get a restraining order, you may need a lawyer to make an application to the court.

— A judge can give a restraining order even if you are not afraid for your personal safety. If the person ignores the order, your lawyer has to start a civil contempt proceeding in court. The police do not enforce civil orders. The person would have to explain to the court why he or she broke the conditions of the order. The judge could order that the person be fined or go to jail until he or she obeys the court order.

Protection order

This is a civil court order issued under provincial family

violence legislation. Not all provinces have such legislation. Where it exists, it provides various emergency and long-term orders to protect victims of family violence. A protection order may give temporary custody of children and the home to the victim, while ordering the abusive person out of the home. It can include conditions such as not allowing any contact.

Some of the following tips apply if a stranger is stalking you, others if an ex-partner is bothering you. You should not use this information in place of seeking police assistance.

Tell others

Tell your supervisor and co-workers. Your workplace may have programs to help deal with harassment. They may be able to screen calls or prevent delivery of unwanted parcels or mail. Ask them never to give out your personal information.

Tell your child's school or day care, and give them copies of any orders that prohibit the non-custodial parent from contacting the child. If a stranger is stalking you, provide a description of the person, the car, the licence plates and so on. Let all of these people know if you have a court order or peace bond and what conditions apply.

Keep personal information private

— Do not use your social insurance number except for banking and income tax forms. It could help someone track you down.

— Remove personal details from things you throw out or recycle.

— At work, remove your nameplate and other personal information, if possible.

Be safe on the telephone

— Consider an unlisted phone number.

— Carry a cell phone for emergency calls.

— Tell your telephone company about your situation.

Ask about tracing calls and security and privacy features like blocking personal information from call displays.

Practise Internet safety

— Be careful about posting personal or private information.

— Check the harassment policies of your Internet Service Provider (ISP).

— Do not use your full name for your user ID, and change your password often.

— Report harassing e-mail or chat room abuse to your ISP. If you know the ISP of the person, tell that ISP too. They can cut off the person's account if it is being used to harass others. Ask about tools to block unwanted communication.

— Do a Web search on cyberstalking. You will find many sites with tips and information. Some can help track down harassers, document their origin and send reports to you or the police.

Do a home security check

— Ask the police to help you do a home security check.

— Be sure your windows and doors are always locked and use deadbolts.

— Change your locks if the person is an ex-partner.

— Consider security features like motion detectors and an alarm system.

Always be alert and have a plan

— Always think about your safety.

— Ask the court for a copy of any restrictions in a court order.

— If possible, do not walk alone and stay on well-lit streets.

— If you are being followed on foot, go somewhere safe (like the nearest store) and call for help.

— Always look around and be aware of what is happening.

— Keep paper and pen on you at all times so you can write down a licence number or other details.

— Sit near others when travelling on a bus or subway, and try not to arrive at your stop early. If you do have to wait around, stay in well-lit areas.

— When travelling in your car, always lock the doors. Plan alternative routes and know how to get to the police or fire station.

— If you are being followed in a car, drive somewhere safe and honk until someone comes to help you.

— Change the route you travel to work or home often.

Information about your case

— Check the status of your case by contacting the police.

— Be sure to use the police file number assigned to your case.

— Stay in touch with the police, victim services and the Crown prosecutor and let them know of any changes to your address or telephone number.

Community Resource List

Create your personal community resource list. In addition to the police, there are a variety of organizations that can offer support or helpful information.

3

Collecting and Using Crime, Violence and Discipline Incident Data

There are two priorities have emerged for public schools in recent years. One is for schools to demonstrate that all children are meeting high academic standards as measured by state assessments. The other is for schools to create an environment that is free of violence and other crimes. These are not separate missions. Children need safe and orderly schools in order to learn. Collecting and using incident data are essential steps for creating safe schools. With good data, it is possible to develop effective prevention and intervention plans. Benefits of data collection include helping schools:

— Improve overall school safety;

— Address specific safety or discipline issues;

— Conserve resources including staff time; and

— Obtain additional resources for school safety.

This document presents the recommendations of the Crime, Violence, and Discipline Task Force on what types of information to collect, why it is important to collect such information, and how it can be used to improve school safety.

"Incidents" are anything from criminal acts, such as robbery, that result in the involvement of law enforcement officials to minor problem behaviors that disrupt the orderly functioning of schools and classrooms, such as tardiness. A single event (e.g., a fight) is one incident regardless of how many perpetrators or victims are involved.

Effective data collection and analysis are powerful tools for creating positive learning climates and are critical activities for schools and school districts nationally. A relational database will also prove useful when responding to state and Federal requests for information. For example, three offices of the U.S. Department of Education presently require significant amounts of information on incidents and disciplinary actions from schools, districts, and states. While these data requests are substantial, they are also subject to change. New education legislation often brings new data collection requirements. The flexibility allowed by a relational database can substantially reduce the amount of time needed to comply with current and future requirements.

Local adaptability is a strength of this data collection model. States and local school districts are encouraged to apply the definitions wherever possible, keeping in mind current state legislation and local school board requirements. While these recommendations are not a Federal mandate, for comparability purposes, the Task Force recommends that consistent definitions be used nationally.

Meeting the Challenges of Data Collection

A safe environment, one that is free of threats and intimidation, provides a climate conducive to learning and teaching. Data collection is an important component in creating such an environment. Nonetheless, there are challenges to data collection. One challenge is accuracy-do the data represent what they are intended to represent?

Other challenges include how interpretation of the data affects school image, especially how data are reported by the media, and costs of collecting data. It is important to ensure confidentiality and protect student and staff privacy. It is necessary to exercise caution when sharing information with staff and other professionals serving schools. In addition, it is especially important to exercise caution when working with the public.

The Federal Family Education Rights and Privacy Act (FERPA) prohibits schools and school districts from releasing most types of information about students. Many states also have legislation regarding the confidentiality of student records and information. The purpose of data collection is to support the mission of schools (i.e., to continue efforts to secure a safe and orderly learning place), and not to create a repressive environment.

Security is a more complicated issue now that many records are stored and transmitted electronically. Schools and school districts need to be sure that their computerized data are appropriately protected from unauthorized electronic access. Records can no longer be secured solely by locking the filing cabinet. Incident data can be used to ensure the following:

— Enhancement of effectiveness and efficiency of successful programs;

— Timely modification or termination of ineffective discipline practices; and

— Provision of more specialized behavior supports that can be arranged quickly for students who display chronic problem behaviors.

Ensuring accuracy

To create safe and orderly places for learning, incident data must be accurate. Staff training and other efforts to ensure the reliability and validity of data are critical.

Collecting Data, provides specific details on the Task Force recommendations for the elements to be included in an incident database. In addition to listing types of incidents, variables are identified and defined. A key feature of the incident database is the ability to interface with student and staff databases. It is important that discipline referrals and disruptive incidents be recorded even when they do not cross the threshold for state-mandated reporting or legal violations. This information can be used to identify trends and link incidents to grade level, location, time of year, or other potentially useful factors.

When designing a database system or purchasing one that is commercially available, users need to evaluate key features, such as whether users will be able to produce all comments necessary to identify problem areas. Problem reports and trend data can be used to set specific goals for preventing problem behavior, develop school improvement programs, and facilitate documentation of progress in addressing school needs.

Training is a critical element of data collection. It is important to train all school staff on what kinds of problem behavior are to be reported to administrators. It is important for administrators to be clear on how incidents are defined, and for both administrators and data entry personnel to understand the specifics of reporting procedures. Some say that statewide training for all school divisions on the implementation of an incident based data collection and reporting procedure, as well as training on the appropriate use of such information for school safety planning and procedures. School level administrators will be better prepared to guide their staff in district discipline policy if they themselves receive training from qualified instructors.

District level administrators can educate school level administrators more effectively regarding state mandates if they have received guidance on the subject. A coordinated, integrated training program will provide both clarity of policy goals and consistency of implementation.

Providing guidance on discipline to administrators takes two forms: (1) training on record keeping and (2) instruction regarding definitions and classification of incidents and disciplinary actions. If school district administrators wish to compare incident data across schools, they need to do more than leave it to untrained school staff to simply choose the incident code that most nearly matches the infraction. Doing so may produce inconsistent data. Even with clear and concise definitions, training at all levels is crucial to ensure data comparability.

Districts may want to consider forming discipline committees to review data, develop and implement plans for training, and revise codes as necessary. Including practice on identifying the types of misbehavior to be recorded would be beneficial. Examples of what does and does not meet the standard for each type of infraction will be important to differentiate among definitions.

Technical assistance staff in Florida provide guidance on incident reporting during regional workshops. School and district administrators are trained on how to categorize incidents and what level of problem behavior meets the threshold for state-mandated reporting. Before developing this program, state staff worked to identify reporting problems, revise and clarify definitions, and develop technical assistance materials such as video clips of examples and "nonexamples" of each type of incident. School and district administrators and law enforcement officials contributed to this process. The state also provides grants to school districts that need additional support to work with their schools on data collection issues. Many districts in Florida follow this model (See Figure 1).

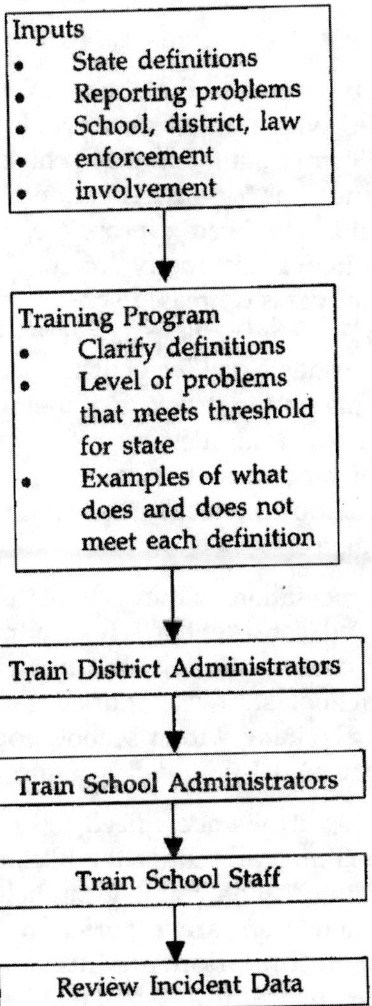

Figure 1. Florida Training Effort

Training is provided to district staff, school administrators, and data clerks. This training addresses:

— Definitions,

— Problem areas, and

— Data uses.

Disorderly conduct that rose to the level of "state reportable" was a significant problem one year in one district. District staff felt that school staff were coding many incidents as "disorderly conduct" when a less serious code would have been appropriate. Training focused on the definition of "disorderly conduct," and the number of reported incidents decreased substantially. Another district found that some principals were recording fights as multiple incidents-one incident for each participant. They held training on the structure of their database, which has separate modules for incident and perpetrator information; thus, the incident itself is recorded in one data file and the information on each perpetrator is recorded in a separate data file.

Documentation within schools is most likely to be accurate and consistent if school administrators or their assistants code infractions, but it is still very important that all school staff are trained regarding prohibited behaviors. Training within schools could follow the state and district model provided in figure 1.

School staff members need to be trained on what to report. Training will reduce the likelihood of inconsistent reporting. In addition, training can help ensure that minor problem behaviors are reported before they escalate. Including information on incident definitions and reporting procedures in teacher handbooks is recommended. Efforts to ensure consistency among staff members in the level of misbehavior that will be tolerated are also important. In addition, regular review of incident reporting and discipline problems at faculty meetings is useful.

Reliability and validity are important components of data collection. The following components ensure that reporting is consistent and that variables measure what they were intended to:

— Clear definitions;

— Handbooks, rules, policies, practices, and data elements aligned with one another;

— Checks for completeness and accuracy;

— Comparison with and contrast to other data sources; and

— Detailed reports.

Training, as discussed earlier, is obviously an important component of ensuring reliability and validity. Before people can be trained, however, it is necessary to adopt clear definitions for incidents and incident elements and to ensure that these variables are consistently defined in student, staff, and parent handbooks and other written instructions.

Decisions on which incidents to include need to be made by the people they affect. Involving stakeholders in the decisionmaking process will generate support for data collection efforts-no effort can succeed without the support of front-line individuals. If data collection decisions are being made at the school level, it is critical to include teachers and other staff on the team that designs the incident-reporting system.

If the decisions are being made at the district level, it is necessary to include school administrators and school staff in the process. If decisions are being made at the state level, it is important to include school and school district administrators in the process. It may also be helpful to include parents and community members on the incident committee. Information that is useful to individual schools may not be useful to the school district as a whole. For example, it may be important for a school to know whether an incident occurred in the locker room or in the cafeteria, but the school district may not need to know this. Similarly, a state may not need to know whether an attendance policy violation consisted of skipping class or forging an absence note.

Communication is essential to ensure reliability and validity. It is critical to clearly describe behaviors that have been defined as infractions in student, staff, and parent handbooks. Students need to know what behaviors are unacceptable before they can be expected to behave appropriately. Staff must know the behaviors for which they are expected to discipline students before they can do so. Finally, parents must be informed about how their children are expected to behave.

Data checks: It is crucial that data be reviewed regularly for completeness and accuracy. It is also necessary to verify that all data elements are being recorded for each incident. During the data review process it is important to examine incident elements being tracked. At the school level, all incidents recorded on paper need to be entered into the incident database.

Staff need to note on each paper reporting form that the incident has been recorded before the form is filed. It is important to establish a system for recording this information to increase the likelihood that information will be recorded as intended. Reviewing paper files to determine whether or not incidents were recorded appropriately may also be useful in managing data entry systems. Assigning a key person the responsibility for oversight of all aspects of incident reporting can improve accuracy.

One way to assess accuracy is to compare a sample of incident forms to what has been recorded in the database for those incidents. When assessing accuracy, it is also important to consider differences from month to month or week to week in the number of each type of incident. If significantly more or fewer "bullying" incidents occurred in one time period than another, it is important to investigate why that is so. If a new bullying prevention program has been implemented, it would be logical for the number of incidents to increase just after the program takes hold.

At that time staff will be more sensitive to the kinds of behavior that are unacceptable, and for incidents to decrease after a program has been in place for some time, as students learn more positive ways of interacting. The data must also "make sense." In other words, did a school really have 10 battery incidents last month, or is someone miscoding another type of infraction?

Other basic data checks include assessing what percentage of students committed rule violations and which violations are the most frequent. An effective database has built-in checks for consistency of data. For example, if a weapon-related incident is recorded, the computer program will automatically prompt for type of weapon.

When analyzing schools within a district, district staff need to ask whether it is reasonable that School A has more "fights" than School B, given differences in enrollment. If not, more training may be required.

Similarly, it will be useful for district and state staff to ask whether it is reasonable that District A has the same number of "fights" as District B, given differences in enrollment. Compare and contrast. It is useful to compare incident data to other sources. Serious infractions can be compared to police reports. Incidents involving injury can be compared to hospital records. Levels of problem behavior identified in self-reported data from student and teacher surveys can be contrasted with the level of problem behavior being recorded in incident databases. For many reasons, rates reported from these sources will differ from school or district databases. However, it is important to investigate significant disparities. For example, if students are reporting very high rates of drug use but there are very few drug infractions recorded, it will be valuable to learn why the difference exists.

It is reasonable to be concerned about how data will be used. Such concerns should not become barriers to effective data collection. Problem behavior will not go away if ignored. Without information on what kinds of problem behavior exist, schools will not be able to take steps to address their problems. It is important that information lead to action, not frustration.

One use of data is to identify students, schools, and school districts in need of additional supports. Schools cannot demonstrate improvement without a way to establish a starting point-an incident database can provide this. Parents and the public want schools to produce well-educated students. Given this focus, it is important to educate the public on the need to invest energy in creating safe and orderly schools.

The premise that an orderly environment is an important factor in student achievement, and that students cannot be successfully engaged in academic work in a disorderly environment, must be communicated to parents, taxpayers, and policymakers. One way to do this is to develop strong media relations. Positive media relations. Working with the media can help schools, districts, and states present data in ways that will help strengthen public support for their data collection and prevention efforts. In "A Short Guide to School Public Relations," some explains that when the facts are known, the vast majority of people are supportive of the efforts of their school leaders. He notes that the time to launch a public relations effort is not during a crisis. A well-designed public relations program aims to prevent problems, not to solve them. Sound public relations efforts can be used to build public support for schools.

The National School Public Relations Association recommends enlisting the media to publicize efforts to promote school safety. Another important strategy is to ensure that all communication contains some form of success story, even when problems are being identified, because this conveys the message that something can be done to improve matters.

Other experts on school public relations recommend that, when school officials are talking with the public, they approach problems as "needs"-that is, to let the public know what is needed to accomplish specific goals, and what the community can expect to gain for its support. If the school needs money to implement prevention programs, the public must know how effective these efforts can be.

Public perception: Before sharing data with people outside the school building, school staff need to be aware of this information. Communicating with school staff is a vital part of safety planning and discipline improvement, and staff members will particularly appreciate receiving timely information directly from administrators. Providing staff members with data on behavior improvement gives them an opportunity to be proud of their accomplishments.

In addition, it is important that they know what problems need to be addressed and that they are involved in deciding how the problems will be addressed. Data can easily be shared at faculty meetings or through school improvement teams. Next, share information with parents.

Presentations to parent/teacher associations and school newsletters are two possible communication tools.

The California Department of Education suggests that, when reporting to the public, administrators stress the positive messages illustrated by the data and how data have been used to develop successful programs. When administrators communicate statistical data in such a positive way, the public is presented with a solvable problem, not an insurmountable dilemma. Presenting data offers an opportunity to form a partnership with law enforcement or other community agencies-another potential resource for schools.

Financing Data Collection

It is likely that there will be costs associated with efforts to clarify definitions; aligning handbooks, rules, policies, and practices; and training staff in what and how to report. However, these initial investments can have great payoffs. One of the most important results would be fewer incidents of problem behavior and a net gain in time spent on the task of learning. There is a strong association between students having academic and behavioral problems.

High levels of problem behavior are associated with early grade retention and grade retention is costly, adding at least the expense of an additional year of school to a child's education. According to the National Center for Education Statistics, per-pupil spending averaged nearly $6,500 nationally for the 1998-99 school year. Implementing a system that allows for early identification of students with serious behavior problems and for early intervention could result in substantial cost savings.

The implementation of a system that assists with the prevention of violence and vandalism will also result in cost savings. In addition, schools with low rates of violence and vandalism are more effective places where more learning occurs. Thus, the rationale for data collection meets educational goals of a safe climate for academic achievement.

Collecting Data

Users may choose to collect some or all variables as best suits their needs. There may also be codes within a variable that are not useful for individual schools, districts, or states. This model was developed to be as inclusive as possible. The items included below are those that could be used to make a difference in the climate of a school, school district, or state. The elements are broken into four categories:

- — Information about the incident itself-for example, when it occurred;
- — Perpetrator data;
- — Victim data; and
- — Information about the disciplinary action taken.

Incidents often involve more than one perpetrator, victim, and/or disciplinary action. Relational databases allow users to record any number of components without requiring that the number of components be predetermined by the application developer and therefore limited. For example, perhaps a fight occurs involving 10 perpetrators. If the incident database comprises a single data table which contains three perpetrator fields, it will not permit the school to record all the perpetrators' information in the same entry. However, if the database has a separate perpetrator table, users may simply record an entry for each perpetrator, linking the offenders to the incident with the incident identifier field. Similarly, it is likely that there will be incidents that involve multiple victims or that result in multiple disciplinary actions. Allowing for links from the victim and perpetrator modules to the student and staff databases will simplify data entry. Allowing all disciplinary actions for an incident to be recorded will permit complete review of the frequency with which particular penalties are applied and their relationship to future outcomes.

It is useful to collect victim data. Some people would argue that this is unnecessary as the victim did nothing wrong. However, if collected, this information can be useful in identifying patterns of victimization. In addition to their responsibility to take appropriate action against those who cause victimization, schools and districts have a responsibility to support the victims themselves. This includes prevention programs and other actions to prevent discrimination, harassment, and other problem behaviors. Victim data will facilitate this.

In many schools, staff complete one "incident referral" form for each participant in an incident. In such a school for the situation previously described involving 10 perpetrators, 10 referral forms would be generated. As noted above, a relational database will allow the information from all 10 forms to be linked by the same incident identifier.

The discussion in the remainder of this chapter presumes that a relational database linking victim and perpetrator elements to student and staff databases will be used. It is critical to treat data on incidents, victims, perpetrators, and disciplinary actions as separate categories of information and create separate "modules" or data tables for each category.

Incident Data and Codes

The capture information specific to the incident itself. That is, these variables are used to record what occurred and when. The codes for many variables allow either general or specific information to be collected. The codes are structured so that specific codes can be subsumed under more general codes. This will permit comparability between locales collecting specific information and locales collecting only general information.

Incident Identifier: This is a locally assigned unique identifier to identify each specific incident or occurrence. The same identifier should be used to document the entire incident even if it included multiple offenses and multiple offenders. This is one of the key fields that link incident records to perpetrator, victim, and disciplinary action data. In addition to comprising a unique incident code, this variable could include the following elements:

— School year,

— School identifier,

— School district identifier, and

— State identifier.

Including the school year is useful when records are maintained for more than one year. By including "location" elements, users can distinguish between incidents reported by multiple jurisdictions. The school identifier needs to be included when incident data are reported from the school to the school district. This variable could be a local school district code, the code assigned by the state, or the code assigned by some Federal calcualtions.

The school and school district identifier needs to be included when incident data are collect from school districts to their state offices of education. The district identifier could be the state's code for the district or the code assigned by some Federal surveys such as the Common Core of Data (CCD). A state identifier would need to be included only if incident data are reported to the Federal Government. The level of detail included in this variable will be determined by individual needs.

School number: This number is assigned by the school district or state for the school where the incident occurred. If the incident occurs during an activity or on transportation that is sponsored by the school, district, or state and not attached to a particular school, use a code that is not already assigned to a reporting unit. For example, 9s can be used to capture these "other" situations. Thus, if the state-assigned school code is a four-digit variable, use the code "9999." If a school identifier is included in the incident identifier, as discussed above, it need not be included separately.

Incident date: Use this variable to identify the date when the incident occurred. Allow two digits to capture the day, two digits to capture the month and four digits to capture the year: MM-DD-YYYY.

Time: This variable identifies when the incident occurred and whether or not it occurred during school hours. It is important to record specific information about when an incident occurred. For example, instead of simply recording that an incident occurred during school hours, noting that an incident took place while students were in transit between regular classes or during lunch would make the information more useful.

Rather than recording the exact time of the incident, using descriptors may be more meaningful, as the exact time an incident occurred would not be meaningful outside of the school building-while 8:15 a.m. might be "before school hours" on one campus, it could be "during class" at another. Using these descriptors permits greater comparability across schools and districts. Additionally, given that over the course of the school year adjustments to the school schedule do occur, while 9:00 a.m. might be "during class" most of the time, on the day of a particular incident it may be "before class." Specific time descriptors will be useful if users are trying to identify when problem behavior is most likely to occur.

Although specific descriptors are recommended, this may not be useful for all schools and districts. For this reason, the coding structure permits the more specific codes that describe exactly when "during school hours" an incident occurred to be subsumed under the general "during school hours" code. Thus, two locales need not both use specific codes for all incidents during school hours to be comparable.

Location (Where): This variable identifies where the incident occurred. The primary codes for this variable capture whether the incident occurred on or off the school campus. Again, record specific information about where an incident occurred. For example, rather than simply recording that an incident occurred on campus, record that it took place in a classroom. Specific location descriptors will be useful if users are trying to identify where problem behavior is most likely to occur.

Facilities Code: This variable is intended for school-specific codes that capture precise information on the location where the incident occurred. For example, a school might record class number, hall number, or school bus number. This information will be most useful if schools plot incident locations, but the data may not be necessary for all schools. The codes for this variable are to be user-defined.

Cost: If the incident resulted in a quantifiable monetary loss for any entity involved, identify and record the value of that loss. Cost may be reported by specific dollar amount or range. For example, if vandalism of a school facility results in having repairs made, the value of those repairs should be reported. In addition, the value of personnel resources used for repairs or consumed by the incident should be recorded here. Also record the value of stolen items here.

Reporter: This variable is used to identify the individual who reported the incident. The codes given below permit very specific coding of the individual reporting the incident. Again, individual schools and districts may find that capturing such detailed information is not useful. If that is the case, use code 100 to record that a student reported the incident, rather than codes 110 or 120 to describe exactly what type of student reported the incident. Thus, to be comparable, two locales need not both use the specific codes since all "100s" represent students.

Reporter ID: This variable allows users to record pre-existing school or district staff and student identifiers, when the individual who reported the incident is a student or staff member. This allows descriptive information about the individual to be linked to the incident via the student or staff database.

Weapon Type: This variable is used to identify the type of weapon used during an incident. The Federal Gun-Free Schools Act requires states to report the number of students expelled for bringing firearms to school by type of firearm. The following codes permit detailed coding of the type of weapon used in the incident.

Reported to Law Enforcement: The incident should be coded as reported to law enforcement if the school resource officer or any other law enforcement official was notified about the incident, regardless of whether official action was taken.

Related Elements: Related elements capture supplemental information about incidents. Use these codes when the primary offense is more serious in nature than alcohol or drug, etc. offenses, but includes one of the elements described below.

This information will be useful in expanding the understanding of the scope of these specific types of problems. These elements should be used to describe whether an incident was related to alcohol, drugs, or gang activity, hatemotivated, or weapon-related. For example, if a student committed vandalism while under the influence of alcohol, alcohol was not the primary offense, but the incident was alcohol-related.

When it is unknown whether an incident was related to any of these elements, code the incident as not related. For the purpose of determining the scope of "alcohol" problems, for example, being uncertain whether or not the incident was alcohol-related or knowing that it was not alcohol-related are effectively the same thing.

Alcohol-related: The incident is alcohol-related if those involved in the incident were under the influence of alcohol at the time of the incident or if there is evidence that they had been drinking, based on testing or investigation of a police officer at the scene, or if the incident is somehow related to possession, use, or sale of alcohol. Do not report "Yes" here if the main offense during the incident was possession, use, or sale of alcohol.

Drug-related: The incident is drug-related if those involved in the incident were under the influence of drugs at the time of the incident, based on testing or investigation done by police as a result of the incident, or if the incident is somehow related to possession, use, or sale of drugs. Do not report "Yes" here if the main offense during the incident was possession, use, or sale of drugs.

Gang-Related: The incident is gang-related if it is gang-motivated or if gang membership caused the incident or contributed to actions that occurred during the incident. For example, an incident of vandalism or robbery might be part of an initiation into a gang, or a fight might be caused by gang rivalry. Report an incident as gang-related only if certain that gang membership contributed to the incident.

Hate-related: The incident is hate-related if it is motivated by hate due to some characteristics or perceived characteristics of the victim including race, gender, religion, color, sexual orientation, ethnicity, ancestry, national origin, political beliefs, marital status, age, social and family background, linguistic preference, or disability. Any act, or attempted act, is hate-related if it is designed to cause physical injury, emotional suffering, or property damage through intimidation, harassment, racial/ethnic slurs and bigoted epithets, vandalism, force, or the threat of force, motivated all or in part by hostility to some real or perceived characteristic of the victim.

Weapon-related: This includes incidents where any of those involved in tne incident possessed or used a weapon during the incident or the incident was somehow related to possession, use, or sale of weapons. Do not report "Yes" here if the main offense during the incident is possession, use, or sale of weapons. In that case code this as weapons possession (code 3700).

Incident Codes: This section presents recommendations for categorizing behavior incidents into specific incident codes. These codes are presented alphabetically. Users may wish to assign a hierarchy so that the code assigned describes the most serious component of the incident. A hierarchy could be based on capturing the type of problem behavior that causes the most injury or greatest loss of property, or it could be based on locally defined parameters.

As noted earlier, some incident codes are structured so that one can choose to record specific types of violations. Also as noted above, only record specific information if it will be useful. More specific information on certain types of misbehavior might be of use to a school or district. The use of subcodes as necessary will meet these needs. In some cases, it may be difficult to determine the code that most accurately describes an incident. For example, a fight could be construed as a more serious or less serious incident. Training staff on how to apply definitions is important to accurate reporting. Similarities are identified below with references to other codes that may describe an incident more accurately.

Perpetrator Information

These variables identify the type of perpetrator (offender) involved in the incident.

Perpetrator: The codes provided below permit very specific recording of the type of individual(s) who committed the incident. Again, individual schools and districts may find that capturing such detailed information is not useful. If that is the case, use code 100 to record that a student was the perpetrator rather than codes 110 or 120 to describe exactly what type of student committed the incident. Thus, to be comparable, two locales need not both use the specific codes because all "100s" represent students.

Perpetrator ID: This variable allows coding of pre-existing school or district staff and student identifiers, when the perpetrator is a student or staff member. This will allow descriptive information about the individual to be linked to the incident via the student or staff database.

Perpetrator Injury: Record whether or not the perpetrator was physically injured, and if so, identify whether the injury was major or minor.

Victim Information

These variables identify the type of victim involved in the incident. Recording this information in a separate data table permits links to the incident module and student and staff databases. This will facilitate the coding of multiple victims.

Victim: The codes provided below permit very specific recording of the type of individual(s) victimized in an incident. Again, individual schools and districts may find that capturing such detailed information is not useful. If that is the case, using code 100 records that a student was victimized. It is not necessary to code 110 or 120 to describe exactly what type of student was victimized. Thus, to be comparable, two locales need not both use the specific codes, since all "100s" represent students.

Victim ID: This variable allows coding of pre-existing school or district staff and student identifiers when the victim is a student or staff member. This allows descriptive information about the individual to be linked to the incident via the student or staff database.

Victim Injury: Record whether or not the victim was physically injured and, if so, identify whether the injury was major or minor.

Discipline Information

The codes described in this section are those necessary to capture information about the outcome of the incident, including the type of punishment that was assigned and its duration. The database structure described above permits multiple disciplinary actions to be recorded for each incident-not only more than one per incident, but also more than one per participant.

Disciplinary action: This variable identifies the consequences of the incident to the student(s) involved in the incident. It is a comprehensive list and was developed to be as inclusive as possible. Some codes may not be appropriate to individual schools and districts given local policies and procedures. Use only those that apply.

Note that, when data is requested by the U.S. Department of Education, for example, multiple codes might fit each disciplinary action specified by a data collection. To illustrate, the Office for Civil Rights collects information on out of-school suspensions. Disciplinary actions described as change of placement may be categorized as out-of-school suspensions by some jurisdictions and would be reported as such for those localities.

These codes are presented alphabetically. Individual schools, districts, or states may wish to assign a hierarchy based on locally defined parameters for severity of the penalty.

Start Date of Disciplinary Action: This variable is used to record the date on which the disciplinary action begins. Use two digits to capture the day, two digits to capture the month, and four digits to capture the year: MM-DDYYYY.

End date of disciplinary action: This variable is used to record the date through which the disciplinary action is in effect. Use two digits to capture the day, two digits to capture the month, and four digits to capture the year: MMDD-YYYY.

Duration of disciplinary action: This variable is used to record the length, in school days, of the disciplinary action. Use decimal places for fractions of school days.

The variable records whether or not any of the disciplinary actions taken against a student were imposed as a consequence of the incident were related to a special education manifestation hearing.

Related to zero tolerance policy variable records whether or not any of the disciplinary actions taken against a student were imposed as a consequence of state or local zero tolerance policies.

Full year expulsion expulsion with or without services for a period of one full year. Shortened expulsion with or without services that is shortened to a term of less than one year by the superintendent or chief administrator of a school district.

The Cycle of Data Collection

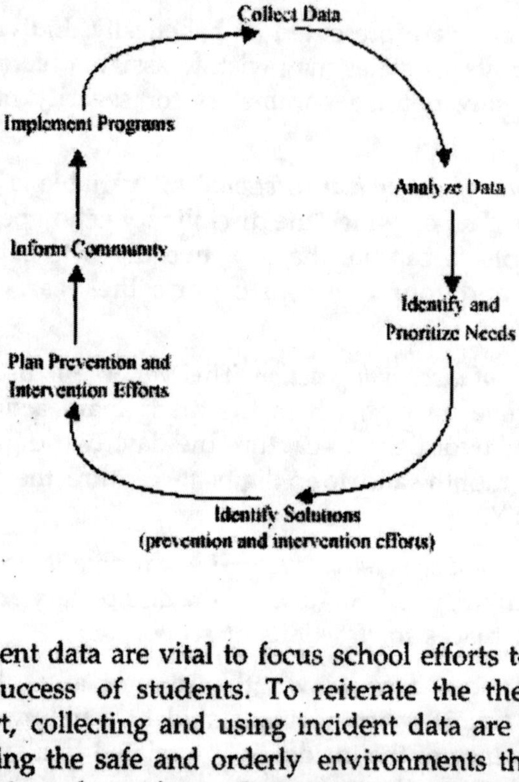

Incident data are vital to focus school efforts to maximize the success of students. To reiterate the theme of this report, collecting and using incident data are essential to creating the safe and orderly environments that students need in order to learn. Data are important to help:

— Replace hunches with facts,

— Identify the causes of problems,

— Assess needs so that services can be targeted,

— Determine whether goals are being accomplished,

— Understand the impact of prevention and intervention, and

— Answer community questions regarding the results of their investment.

While a comprehensive incident database makes it easier to manage resources and complete state and Federal incident reports, the most important reason to collect data is to facilitate activities that promote learning. Using incident data to make a difference in schools is a cyclical activity. Without accurate data, it is difficult to take appropriate steps to create climates conducive to learning.

Communicating with the community about prevention needs is especially important. Parents, community members, and funders need facts to make informed decisions about the needs of schools. Legislatures and community foundations have targeted millions of new dollars for prevention and intervention efforts after learning about incident data. For example, Pennsylvania, responding to increasing concerns about violence in schools, awarded nearly 9 million dollars in safe-school grants to school districts across the state to strengthen their violence prevention programs and to make schools safer.

Similarly, the Colorado Trust in 1999, recognizing the need for violence prevention efforts, committed 1 million dollars over 3 years to support the Safe Communities - Safe Schools Initiative in 8 schools and school districts. This process is a never-ending story. Along the way, it will be necessary to address the challenges of data collection such as ensuring accuracy and concerns about school image.

Accurate data can be collected when a comprehensive database is developed and staff are given training about what types of problem behaviors are to be reported.

Actions to ensure reliability and validity are important. Such actions include clearly defining problem behavior, performing data checks, and comparing and contrasting incident data with other sources. While it is reasonable to be concerned about how data will be used, proactively communicating with the public regarding school needs and educating the public about the need to invest resources in efforts to promote school safety are critical to gaining support.

In closing, it is insufficient to simply collect incident data. Rather, collecting incident data is the beginning of working towards school improvement. It is important for schools, school districts, and states to use that data to develop plans for action in order to make a difference and improve the teaching and learning environment.

4

Police and the Public

The Government's aim is to put people at the centre of public services. With increasing investment, the public rightly has increasing expectations of the quality of the services it receives. Providers of services across the public and private sectors are facing mounting external pressures from a more demanding consumer culture and an environment where communities are becoming increasingly diverse, complex and mobile. Policing is no exception.

Added to these pressures for change is the place occupied by the police service in our shared idea of community. The local police serve as a focus for communities' sense of safety and security. As well as those who have direct contact with the police, everyone benefits from the services provided by the police on a daily basis. As such the police service has a unique value and importance to the public.

But the relationship between the public and the police is not only critical to people's feelings of safety, fear of crime or confidence. It is also essential to the continued effectiveness of the police in tackling crime and disorder and bringing offenders to justice. Bringing about safer and more secure communities is dependent on the co-operation and support of members of the public, for example, by people providing information leading to the arrest of criminals involved in dealing drugs and gun crime and acting as witnesses when cases come to court. Local communities are often best placed to find the most appropriate and long-term solutions to problems of crime and anti-social behaviour.

Forging a new relationship between the police and the public - in which there is active collaboration between the police, their partners and citizens in the delivery of policing services -is the underlying principle on which our proposals are based. We recognise that effective policing will only be sustained over the long term when it is citizen-focused - responsive to people's needs and performed as a shared undertaking with the active involvement of the public. But in order to engage and be involved, people must have a basic confidence that they are guaranteed high standards of service; that policing in their area reflects and responds to their needs; and that they have genuine opportunities to become involved on their own terms. The Government recognises that there is already much good work underway in a number of forces that is proving successful. We want to build on this and bring all forces up to the same high standard.

Tackling crime and reassuring the public go hand in hand - to pursue one at the expense of the other may work in the short term but over the long term is unsustainable. We want a situation where a two-way exchange of information between the police and the public leads to improvements in crime reduction and ever increasing levels of trust and confidence. There are real wins here for the police, the public and society in general.

Neighbourhood Policing for Today's World

Revitalising the policing of neighbourhoods for today's world is central to the Government's approach to improving policing in this country. Despite year on year reductions in crime, the public's fear of crime remains too high. Many people are, understandably, not convinced that crime is going down if they do not see and experience effective and responsive policing themselves - in their neighbourhoods and communities; and when they have contact with the police. A positive experience of policing is also vital to building people's trust and confidence in the police service itself.

But unlike previous community policing initiatives, the new style of neighbourhood policing being advanced by the Government in partnership with the police service will not just be about delivering public reassurance, as important as that is. Excellent police forces today can and should be about reassuring the public and preventing and detecting crime.

And importantly for the Government, its approach to neighbourhood policing involves harnessing the energies of local communities and partners to exchange information and work together to continue to reduce crime and anti-social behaviour and improve the number of crimes detected and offences brought to justice. Establishing effective and responsive neighbourhood policing is essential to making this happen. How will this approach to neighbourhood policing operate in practice?

The Government recognises that a number of police forces in England and Wales are already putting in place what is needed for a successful neighbourhood policing approach. We want to build on this good practice.

The critical starting point for the Government is forces having dedicated teams of police officers and community support officers, working in concert with wardens and other members of what is sometimes referred to as the 'extended police family' to provide a visible and accessible presence in communities. Ongoing workforce modernisation pilot schemes are providing valuable evidence of the impact so-called 'mixed economy' teams can have in neighbourhoods and beyond. We want such teams to develop a genuine sense of being responsible for and 'owning' their local areas.

This means the police involving communities in negotiating priorities for action and, together with partners and the communities themselves, finding lasting solutions to local problems. We talk about this kind of engagement further in paragraphs 3.45 onwards below. But more than this, we are clear that neighbourhood policing for today's world must be intelligence-led, which involves the systematic adoption and application of the National Intelligence Model. So along with greater accessibility and responsiveness to people's concerns and needs, the roll-out of neighbourhood policing will mean a more proactive, problem-orientated approach being taken to local issues.

The Government has been engaged in a programme of pilot initiatives and research to understand the essential elements of a successful neighbourhood policing approach. We have also been able to draw on the experience of forces both in this country and abroad. Neighbourhood policing will not mean a one-size fits all approach, but we believe that effective models will share the following features:

— dedicated resources for neighbourhoods which include the extended police family, but where numbers, staffing mix, skills and powers available are appropriate to the particular needs of the neighbourhood;

— an emphasis on local problem solving with mechanisms in place to identify and respond to neighbourhood level priorities and to draw in additional resources from other levels and partners where necessary;

— engagement with communities, using a range of methods appropriate to the communities concerned;

— a focus on public involvement not only in identifying problems but in prioritising action and shaping and participating in solutions, along with police and partners; and

— mechanisms in place to target resources at local priorities and to hold police and partners to account for tackling neighbourhood problems.

Effective neighbourhood policing is therefore about more than satisfying a public desire for more 'bobbies on the beat' and cannot be seen as an activity that stands in isolation from the rest of policing. To be successful, neighbourhood policing needs to apply the same intelligence-led approach that has been so successful at tackling volume crime and serious organised crime. People who are living within communities blighted by violent or drug-related crime know that it is not just 'quality of life issues' that concern local communities.

There is not a quick fix. Their priorities often link directly to policing issues which cross force boundaries such as drug importation and trafficking. Many of the problems facing communities have existed for decades and will take time to resolve. But putting in place dedicated neighbourhood teams can build up relationships of trust with local communities over time. These teams are ideally placed to monitor issues and tensions within the community. We see an essential part of their role to be gathering community intelligence, which must be fed into the National Intelligence Model process.

To be successful - and to avoid replicating the problems with previous approaches to community policing - the Government is clear that its approach to neighbourhood policing must not be seen as some kind of bolt-on or distinct activity by police forces. Effective neighbourhood level policing requires proper integration with other policing functions such as first contact, response, investigation and major crime work. It will therefore need the wholesale commitment of forces to put in place an infrastructure to support it.

Government support for neighbourhood policing

The Government's ongoing programme of reform is already providing the building blocks for the kind of neighbourhood policing approach set out in this paper. We have, for example, introduced the role of community support officer and made other changes in terms of civilianising police posts and reducing bureaucracy to free up frontline officers' time. The police pay reforms agreed in 2002 provide a way for forces to reward staff in particular posts - like community or neighbourhood officers - in order to attract and, crucially, retain people in those important roles -where continuity is vital.

Some police forces have already committed themselves to neighbourhood policing and they, and their communities, are starting to feel the impact. But elsewhere, effective and responsive neighbourhood policing is not business as usual. We want communities across the country to benefit from this style of policing and believe that, in addition to investment, the spread of neighbourhood policing requires the development of a supportive infrastructure and an understanding of new tactics. Effective management of a wide range of resources to meet local needs, for example, is key to ensuring the successful and sustainable implementation of the kind of dedicated neighbourhood policing approach set out in this chaper. In terms of support, the Government will therefore:

— set out joint guidance on neighbourhood policing for forces with the Association of Chief Police Officers and the National Centre for Policing Excellence early in 2005;

— put in place a programme to help forces implement neighbourhood policing and make sure that the highly skilled role of neighbourhood officers is recognised, valued and trained in the same way as other specialists within the police service;

— support the roll-out of neighbourhood policing with substantial investment through the new Neighbourhood Policing Fund. We will deliver 25,000 CSOs and wardens by 2008; and

— run a national community policing

Investing in Neighbourhood Policing

The Government has already injected £50m of new money this year to provide what is, in effect, the first round of the Neighbourhood Policing Fund. This will mean an additional 2,000 CSOs will be recruited by the end of March 2005. We will deliver 25,000 CSOs and wardens by 2008. Forces will receive continuation funding and will be required to maintain police officer numbers to be eligible for Neighbourhood Policing Fund money. The Fund will pay for existing CSOs and for measures being funded already to increase the capacity of the special constabulary. Beyond this, the Neighbourhood Policing Fund is intended to be a flexible investment fund to support the implementation of neighbourhood policing. Unlike the Crime Fighting Fund, the additional money in the Neighbourhood Policing Fund will not simply be used on a "money for people" basis.

Police authorities and forces will be invited to set out their plans for the implementation of neighbourhood policing, including a commitment to the number of CSOs they will recruit. But how they use money from the

Neighbourhood Policing Fund to achieve this will be up to them. The Government will set out the full details of requirements for applications to the Neighbourhood Policing Fund in 2006/07 and 2007/08 in mid 2005.

Reducing bureaucracy

As part of drive on neighbourhood policing and supporting the development of a more responsive police service, the Government remains committed to reducing the administrative burdens and eliminating unnecessary paperwork and inefficient working practices that keep officers away from the communities they serve. We want to empower officers and equip them to spend time in their core roles - tackling crime and providing reassurance to the public. We are already making progress:

— over 7,700 forms have been made obsolete across all 43 forces;

— all 43 forces now undertake video identity parades to speed up the identification of suspects. It is estimated that it takes 66% less time for a uniformed officer to carry out a video identity parade than a live one. They greatly reduce bureaucracy, are welcomed by forces and, over five years, will represent an overall saving of £143m to the police service;

— over 72,000 police officers and staff are now using the new generation of Airwave radios operationally in 40 forces, and 20 forces are using mobile information. This allows officers to cut down on the amount of time spent returning to the station and is making a significant difference to everyday policing;

— the national roll out of the penalty notice for disorder scheme was completed in April 2004. Over 30,000 such notices had been issued by the end of September 2004, each one representing a file for court which did not have to be prepared. It is estimated that around 90 minutes is saved per ticket. The scheme is being extended to build on its success. A further 10 offences, including criminal damage and theft, have been added, with CSOs being able to issue penalty notices for disorder for all the new offences, except theft. The scheme is also being extended to tackle disorderly and nuisance offending by juveniles. From 20 January 2005, 16 and 17 year olds will be able to be issued with penalty notices for disorder. We have pased legislation to enable the scheme to be extended to juveniles aged 10 to 15 years of age and pilots are expected to start later in 2004;

— 198 Livescan Units, which enable electronic fingerprint images to be taken from people instantly, are in use in 35 forces;

— we are investing £13m over two years into 10 pilot projects to test out new ways of using police staff to carry out station-based jobs traditionally performed by officers. For example, we have invested £2.5 million in new investigation teams in Surrey which will include administrators and investigative officers, allowing detective constables to do less routine paperwork and concentrate on work which is better suited to their skills, experience and training; and

— the recommendations of the new Sentencing Guidelines Council, if implemented, will reduce sentence reductions only for those who plead guilty at the courtroom door with very large potential benefits in terms of reduced file preparation where that leads to earlier guilty pleas; and

— on 1 September 2004, a Policing Bureaucracy Gateway began to operate at the Home Office and the Association of Chief Police Officers. This identifies, challenges and influences the demands made by new policies, legislation and procedures that affect the police service. We will encourage individual forces in parallel to set up their own gateways to influence the demands imposed locally.

The Government is providing practical assistance to forces in their work to reduce bureaucracy through the appointment, in January 2004, of an assistant chief constable whose responsibility is to visit forces to spread good practice, raise awareness and, where necessary, challenge existing practices. We are setting up an actionline for officers to raise any questions they have relating to bureaucracy. This will help to engage frontline officers in the work that is being undertaken nationally in this area. We will ensure that officers' ideas are followed up and we will publish the outcome. We have also set up an annual Reducing Bureaucracy Awards Scheme with the Police Federation, which encourages frontline officers to come up with suggestions for reducing bureaucracy. The first awards ceremony took place at the Police Federation Conference in May 2004.

Reducing bureaucracy is making an important contribution to increasing the time available for frontline duties. This is crucial in terms of getting officers out into communities. Increasing the proportion of time which police officers spend on frontline duties - a priority on which the police service has worked with us for some time - could deliver a substantial proportion of the overall 3% efficiency target set by the 2004 Spending Review settlement.

Exploiting new technology, more effective deployment of officers and more effective use of police staff will also help to increase the amount of frontline policing. Other efficiency gains will be delivered through more efficient working and commercial practices. Reform of the Home Office will also help to reduce burdens on the service that can detract from efficiency. Like our overall programme itself, this is reform for a purpose - which is about helping to make policing more effective for all our communities.

The Home Office is working in partnership with the Association of Police Authorities and the Association of Chief Police Officers in a new efficiency implementation group to identify and implement the best ways to increase value for money in policing. Greater value for money will enable the service to devote the greatest possible level of resources to protecting and serving the public.

Police forces and authorities are required to include in their annual policing plans efficiency plans which set out the value for money gains they intend to achieve. We expect them, as part of their planning process, to consider what action they can take to minimise bureaucratic burdens. This is in line with the duty on police authorities to maintain an effective and efficient police force for their area.

Underpinning our approach to neighbourhood policing, the Government sees the need to improve the responsiveness and customer service culture of all police forces in England and Wales. The proposals for making improvements are set out below.

The Government is clear that providers of public services, including the police, must ensure that services are citizen-focused - designed around the people who use and receive their services not the professionals who work within them. The experience of other organisations has shown that such a change can deliver improved outcomes and efficiencies. There is evidence, for example, that witnesses who are more satisfied with their experience of the Criminal Justice System are more likely to be prepared to give evidence in the future.

Many forces have found that focusing on the needs of the people who use their services can also reduce bureaucracy and improve efficiency. It does not necessarily follow that there is a cost to making services more responsive to people's needs. Indeed making this change can bring considerable benefits. Whilst much work is already underway within forces to make their services more citizen-focused, making this 'business as usual' will require significant cultural and organisational change, as well as the development of new skills and capabilities within the workforce.

The Government sees its role as putting in place a framework that will drive and support changes. But we are clear that these need to be led and developed at local level by police forces, police authorities and their local partners who will need to embrace a cultural shift towards being more open and accessible to the public and be willing to listen and adopt new approaches to deliver more effective local services.

A new culture of customer service and responsiveness

Investment in record levels of police numbers and the hard work police forces, police authorities and their partners have done to reduce crime in recent years will be undermined if people's confidence is damaged by a poor experience when they have contact with the police. Last year, 44% of the public had some form of direct contact with the police. Nearly a third of the public initiated that contact themselves - not only victims and witnesses of crime, but also those seeking advice and information. Research has shown that personal experience, and that of family and friends, is the most important influence on public views of the police and that the experience of contact will shape public views of the police service for a long time to come. So in order to help secure public support and confidence, it is vital that people's experience of contact with the police is a good one - wherever that contact takes place.

How people rate the contact they have had with the police has a strong impact on perceptions of local police performance in general. Unlike the health service and education, the more contact people have with the police the less satisfied they are likely to be with the service. Recent figures show police were more likely to be rated as doing a good job by people who had no contact with them over the previous year than those who did. Those who have positive perceptions of their contact with the police are significantly more likely to have a favourable impression of the police's performance in their local area than those who are dissatisfied with their police contact.

But there is nothing inevitable about this relationship. Forces which are making improvements to the customer service they provide are seeing rising satisfaction as a result. For example, Lancashire Constabulary discovered that by finding out what is important to the public when they contact them and making small changes in the way they do things as a result, they could greatly increase the satisfaction of the people who used their services. Simply by not making promises they could not keep - by telling non-emergency callers how long it would take for an officer to arrive for example - satisfaction has increased. This shows that getting the quality of service provided to the public right matters.

Guaranteed standards of service to the public

We want to see this responsiveness to customer needs replicated everywhere and ensure that all members of the public have a consistent, high quality of service that meets their needs whenever they are in contact with the police.

This should be irrespective of where, how or for what reason that contact takes place. We have been working with the Association of Chief Police Officers to develop national standards that will set out the quality of service the police service is committed to providing to the public whenever they have contact with them. Every force will have these standards in place by the end of 2006 and will agree in a 'Contract' with their communities how these can be built on locally, to reflect the particular needs of the communities they serve.

As a result of implementing the standards it will be easier for the public to contact the police, the way that initial enquiries from the public are dealt with will be improved and victims will be kept better informed about the progress of their case. Standards will also cover the way people can expect to be treated by police staff and ensure that all forces have a proper system in place to monitor the quality of the service provided, and act on any feedback received from the public about their experience of contact.

The Government believes that improving the relationship with the public will be as beneficial to the police as it will to the public. As a result of implementing the customer service standards, frontline staff will be better supported to deal effectively with the public, forces will have a more accurate understanding of demand patterns, improved systems in place to manage demand and a better flow of intelligence from the public. All of this will help forces target resources more effectively.

The Government is aware that forces are already taking steps to improve the customer service they provide and there are many good initiatives underway. But we want to ensure that all forces are brought up to the level of the best. This will require a systematic approach on the part of forces to understanding the needs of the people who use their services and redesigning and delivering services with those needs in mind.

This approach recognises that good customer service is not just about being polite to people - it is about employing the methods that other private and public sector organisations use because it makes good business sense. As part of a process of change, the Government believes that police forces will need to put in place the techniques that have been developed in other sectors, such as:

— an evidence based understanding of demand patterns and the needs of users and wider public - knowing not making assumptions;

— setting clear expectations for staff on the quality of service to be provided;

— quality control - follow up and monitoring of standards that reflect public needs;

— systems and business processes in place to support a citizen focused service;

— a performance culture that focuses on public satisfaction and recognises the quality issues as well as the things that are easier to measure;

— use of marketing and communications techniques to support the development of a better relationship with the public and manage expectations.

Improving access to services

We want to see increasing choice in the way that services are accessed by the public. Forces will need to build on these locally to continue to develop the range of ways the public can access services and ensure that these are appropriate to the needs of the communities they serve.

Many forces are now working with partners to adopt a joint approach to dealing with problems that require a multi-agency response, for example, the use of multi-agency One Stop Shops, council offices, post offices, health centres and libraries.

Police forces have reported year on year increases in the number of calls they receive from the public - the majority of which are not emergencies, or even reports of a crime. Many are not about things that the police can deal with alone or even at all, but people have called the police because they do not know which agency or organisation they should be contacting or what other help is available to them.

Sometimes the nature of the problem means that dealing with it requires the collaboration of a number of different agencies and there may not be an easy way to get this to happen. Not only does this mean that it is taking longer for the public to find someone who can help them, but when people call the police as a last resort it adds to the pressures on the 999 system. Frontline officers are often sent to deal with problems that could have been resolved over the phone or dealt with by another agency or organisation much earlier on.

The Government has made a commitment to introduce a single non-emergency number, and we have secured with Ofcom agreement in principle to the provision of a universally applicable three-digit number. Public consultation has revealed strong support for the idea. We are currently considering which range of services the public would most benefit from having a single point of access to, and which would alleviate the demands on public services, particularly police and local authorities.

Many calls made to the police are actually about anti-social behaviour - noisy neighbours, abandoned cars, gangs of youths, graffiti and flytipping - and may require actions by local authorities as well as the police themselves. Shared access can harness more effectively the enforcement powers of both the police and their partner agencies, to ensure that the general public receives a more seamless and satisfactory service.

The Government will build on the success of the together Action Line to provide a direct single non-emergency telephone number for the public which will deal with non-emergency issues of policing, crime and anti-social behaviour. Our aim -depending on the results of a feasibility study - is to have the core of the system in place by the end of 2006. Initially this will be able to resolve some calls over the phone, provide advice on certain matters and where that cannot be done, direct callers to the right person to speak to. We are scoping how this can be rolled out to directly link up with forces, local authorities and other relevant services when they have the right systems in place to do so.

The issue of non-emergency calls demonstrates how the better management of public contact is not just about getting it right for the public but it is also about getting it right for frontline officers. If calls are not assessed and graded correctly and if accurate and relevant information and history is not captured from callers so that officers have a good picture of the call they are attending, their job becomes considerably more difficult.

Improving call handling

Improving the way that calls to the police are dealt with is a particular priority for the public. People's first contact is particularly important in shaping their views of the police service.

Some of this is down to having the right resources, technology and staffing - having sufficient capacity to deal with both 999 calls and non-emergency calls and systems in place to resolve problems over the phone; being able to see all the information that is relevant to that call - such as whether someone has called about the same problem many times before - without searching a separate database. But successful callhandling is core not only to the satisfaction of users, but also to the effective investigation of crime and management of intelligence. As such, training for call handlers needs to equip them with skills in customer service and those necessary to fulfill their critical role in assessing and prioritising calls.

But getting call handling right for the public is also about seeing things from the public's point of view, understanding what is important to them and building this into how business is done. What makes the difference is not just how quickly a call is picked up but also the quality of service the caller receives.

To improve the responsiveness and customer service culture across all police forces, the Government will bring together in 2005 a number of projects as part of a national strategy to improve call handling:

— the Association of Chief Police Officers' programme of work to bring all forces up to the same high standard of call handling, which is due to complete in April 2005;

— a thematic inspection on contact management to be carried out during 2005 by Her Majesty's Inspectorate of Constabulary (HMIC); and

— a manual of best practice on the most effective ways to manage calls from the public which will be published following HMICs inspection.

Training, skills and cultural change

The leadership of managers and chief officers in valuing customer service and communicating this to frontline staff will be critical to delivery of a new culture of customer responsiveness. The actions and behaviour of frontline officers and public facing staff are key to maintaining the reputation of the police, and to some extent the Criminal Justice System as a whole. But so too are the actions and decisions of staff in all levels and roles. This requires the building of a culture that values customer service and new skills for all staff within the organisation, and which is reflected in the way that individual performance is assessed and rewarded.

Measuring public satisfaction

To reflect the importance placed on customer service, the Government is changing the way in which police performance is measured to recognise that public satisfaction is an essential element of good performance. We have already introduced new performance indicators that focus on quality of service. From April 2005, the comparative assessment of overall force performance will include the satisfaction of victims of crime about how easy it was to make contact with the police, how they were treated by staff, the actions police officers took and how they were kept informed of progress. We are continuing to develop this work so that the views of victims of anti-social behaviour can also be reflected in assessments of performance.

Engaging the public

The Government regards the involvement of communities in the process of identifying which problems are the priorities, and being part of the solution, as an essential element of a successful neighbourhood policing approach. It is this direct and continuous engagement that can make the difference between an approach that is sustainable and one that is not. There needs to be an emphasis on relationship building, listening and problem solving.

The public are more than users of services, they are stakeholders in the security of their neighbourhoods. So there needs to be a continuous dialogue and two-way exchange of information and views, together with increased opportunities for participation so that people are more involved. Communities must see how their input is being used to inform and change the delivery of policing services. And people should be clear about how to hold to account those who are responsible for policing and community safety.

At present, police authorities have a statutory responsibility to consult the public on local policing priorities. This has most often been done via what are known as Police Community Consultative Groups. However, Home Office research has shown these formal public meetings to be ineffective for strategic consultation on priority setting. While these groups can sometimes be effective as a local problem solving forum, they are often poorly attended and not representative of the whole community. Many authorities have constituted, abandoned or supplemented such groups with other forms of engagement, but progress has been variable within and between authorities. Moving beyond relying on public meetings as a sole form of engagement is a key aim of our reforms.

The Government acknowledges that many police forces and authorities are adopting a range of more innovative and inclusive techniques to engage their communities. But this is not happening everywhere. Recent Home Office research into the role of police authorities in public engagement found a low public awareness of existing police-public consultation arrangements. Whilst there were examples of engagement impacting on policing plans, community relations and service delivery, not all authorities had a strategy for consultation and community engagement and authorities did not generally monitor impact of engagement in any systematic way. The research suggests that the public feel they do not have a say in decisions about policing but do want better communication, information and involvement.

Underpinning our approach to neighbourhood policing and improving the responsiveness of the police, the Government wants to build on community engagement initiatives already underway and ensure that all communities have the same opportunities to have a real say in the way they are policed, get more involved if they want to, and hold relevant agencies to account locally. There are a number of elements to this approach, which we set out below.

Better information to the public

The Government regards the dissemination to the public of better information about community safety and policing as being a necessary first step towards increasing local engagement and accountability. In many respects, people's understanding of the performance of their local police area lags behind that of other public services - such as local authorities, schools and hospitals - where systems have been put in place for informing the public about the relative and comparative performance of the service in question.

We believe that there is clear value in bringing a broad array of information into one concise and accessible document summarising local policing for the public. And we think that every area of the country should benefit from receiving a consistent level of information. We therefore plan to introduce a statutory minimum requirement in terms of what each household can expect to receive in terms of local policing information.

The stakeholders about what the minimum standards will include but our present thinking is that it should cover the following areas:

— an explanation of local policing priorities and how well they have been discharged;

— information on how local policing is led, organised and delivered, and who is accountable;

— a view of comparative policing performance at the most local level possible, showing specific performance in defined areas, trends over time and comparison to peers;

— specific information on how individuals, groups and communities can influence and engage local policing;

— information on ways to give feedback to the police and what has been done to improve services in response to the feedback received;

— a summary assessment from Her Majesty's Inspectorate of Constabulary's perspective on local policing performance;

— information on how police resources are applied; and

— a requirement for the publication to meet the needs of local communities by incorporating specific additional information, diversity or language requirements.

The Government proposes that the minimum standard will make it clear that each household should expect to receive this information at least once a year. Wherever possible, we think that this should be done in partnership with information being provided to the public by other relevant agencies through, for example, local authority newsletters. In a similar vein, we want to improve the information provided by Crime and Disorder Reduction Partnerships (CDRP) to communities. We will link this with the minimum standards set for policing information so that as far as possible, partnerships and the police have the opportunity to rationalise the way both CDRP and policing specific information is provided to the public.

Helping forces engage with the public

The Government will continue to invest in research and support forces to identify principles of good practice on engaging more effectively with communities. Community engagement will increasingly become a core part of the role of many frontline officers and police staff and they will need the knowledge and skills to undertake such engagement effectively. Much of this information and support material already exists, but is not centrally captured in a form that others can easily share. To overcome this, the Government has invited a group of experienced practitioners from police forces and authorities to form the National Practitioner Panel for Community Engagement in Policing to look at how best to support effective engagement. As a result of its work, the Government will be making available new forms of support and advice on how frontline staff can engage more effectively with local communities.

This will include the development of a database of examples of effective practice so that staff can learn from each other's experience. These tools will be accessible to forces and authorities nationwide in early 2005. The Government has also funded three demonstration sites in Merseyside, Cheshire and Northumbria to test more innovative ways of engaging effectively with communities. The results of this work will inform the Panel's strategy and products, and will be widely available for others to share.

But the Government recognises that there is no "one-size-fits-all" approach to community engagement. What works for one community will not necessarily work for another. Effective engagement can only be achieved by matching the right means to a proper understanding of local circumstances. In identifying "what works", police forces and authorities will therefore need to understand not only which engagement strategies are successful, but why - and in what circumstances - they have been successful.

Measuring performance about responding to local priorities

The Government proposes to make changes to the way police performance is measured and inspected so that it reflects the priorities of the public and their views about the policing they have received. This will include the inclusion of measures about local priorities in the Policing Performance Assessment Framework.

Increasing opportunities for engagement

We are making clear our expectations about the responsibility of the police and partners to actively engage the public and respond to concerns at neighbourhood level and work together to tackle these problems. Closer working between the police, partners and the local community will also help ensure that local resources are targeted more effectively to tackle the issues that really matter to the community.

The Government recognises that, in order to do this effectively, agencies must have the flexibility to develop mechanisms that will suit their local circumstances. However, there also needs to be consistency of outcomes and opportunities for the public to participate. Responses to our consultation paper, Policing: Building Safer Communities Together showed strong support for the proposals for providing greater opportunities to influence policing.

These reforms are not about introducing change for its own sake - but to put in place arrangements that will support the greater operational responsiveness on the part of police and partners that comes with neighbourhood policing. There is no substitute for the importance of personal contact, availability, visibility and therefore accessibility of uniformed officers and community support officers.

Familiarity and trust between neighbourhood teams and local people that develops through a known and consistent presence is the best form of communication. And where agreements between local people, police and partners to take action to deal quickly with neighbourhood priorities can be undertaken less formally and with the minimum of bureaucracy, this option should always be taken before recourse to more formal arrangements.

We think nevertheless that there is a strong case for strengthening the statutory responsibilities of agencies to have arrangements in place to actively engage with communities at neighbourhood level and work together to deal with problems that cut across agency boundaries and require a multiagency solution. We propose that existing duties for partnership working under 17 of the Crime and Disorder Act 1998 should be built on, and a joint duty should be placed on the police and local authorities in each CDRP area to ensure they have sufficient arrangements in place to deliver a range of engagement opportunities for local neighbourhoods and to respond to concerns that are raised as a result. We propose the following changes to existing statutory arrangements:

— extending the responsibility on police authorities to secure the implementation of a strategy to engage the community at all levels - including neighbourhoods - within the police area;

— a direct responsibility on the police in partnership with other bodies to put the strategy into place and to have arrangements to respond to neighbourhood level concerns; and

— a requirement for CDRPs to oversee the delivery of neighbourhood level priorities agreed with local communities. This may involve the routine establishment of joint tasking and co-ordination groups that are already in place in some areas.

We do not intend, however, to prescribe what constitutes a neighbourhood in any given area. This is best determined locally, in consultation with local people - although it will need to be at a sufficiently local level i.e. sub-BCU and meaningful to the community.

We will not be prescriptive about the form these arrangements should take, nor do we intend that separate arrangements for policing and community safety necessarily need to be put in place. Wherever possible existing structures that the local authority already has in place, that are working well should be used. A number of different approaches are available including the Community Service Agreements model advocated by the Scarman Trust.

We recognise too that there are innovative approaches to raising resources, such as cofunding from regeneration and social renewal budgets and levies in relation to defined communities, in some parts of the country at a very local level. Kensington New Deal for Communities in Liverpool, for example, employs wardens, which it jointly funds with the local housing association. And citizens served by parish councils or housing associations have democratic mechanisms, which allow them to give their consent to a local charge that can be used to raise funds for improvements to community safety and the local quality of life. We want to look further at whether these kind of co-funding arrangements could be more widespread, with due regard to social equity, accountability and the interests of local council tax payers.

Local Area Agreements

Local Area Agreements will offer greater freedom and flexibility through the amalgamation of funding streams to achieve priority outcomes at local level. Pilot agreements will be running in 21 areas from April 2005. We intend to include a number of approaches such as those mentioned above in the pilot process as a means to increase engagement at neighbourhood level and improve the responsiveness of public services.

The ethos behind Local Area Agreements is that they should not be prescriptive about solutions and processes but rather should enable each area to agree local solutions for local circumstances. These could include locally-determined community engagement outcomes drawing on effective practice models for community engagement.

Increasing the opportunities for local communities to have a greater voice in and influence over local decision-making and the delivery of services is central to the developing 10-year local government strategy. In many areas, local councillors are the people that communities turn to for advice and support and surveys suggest that the public think that the most important role of councillors should be listening to local people. However, some people think that councillors are out of touch with local concerns. We think therefore that as well as ensuring that the police and partners have arrangements in place to actively engage people at the neighbourhood level, there is a case for strengthening the links between local councillors, in the role they play in community safety issues, and the public.

Community advocacy

The Government's recent consultation exercise on police reform revealed strong support from the public for a community advocacy role within communities. We are clear that it is the democratically elected local councillors who should be advocates for their communities and represent the views of the public about the services they receive. But we recognise that some communities are more able to articulate concerns to them than others. The Home Office will therefore work with the Office of the Deputy Prime Minister as part of the Government's local government strategy, to develop a range of ways in which ward councillors can be assisted to act as advocates. This will include helping local councillors to provide better support to citizens who need to access police or other community safety services. They would actively work with communities and empower individuals to find better solutions to their problems and ensure that the voice of local people about the quality of service received is heard and acted on by service providers.

There are a number of possible options. One could be to develop and/or extend the capacity building and liaison role of community safety officers where they exist. They could work to build stronger relationships with community organisations and networks and have a distinct role in communicating local concerns to ward councillors. This would be an extension of the role which many of them are currently playing as part of Crime and Disorder Reduction Partnerships.

Triggers for local action

Communities rely on the police and their partners to use the powers that only they have available to them to keep their communities safe. They need to be given a guarantee that when faced with a problem that requires the use of those powers, action will be taken on their behalf.

The Government does not want to see local communities being left to fend for themselves because they have not been able to get a response from local agencies. Neither do we want the police or local authorities to be left to deal with recurring problems because they cannot get one or more of their partners to take action to resolve them. The Government therefore proposes introducing a specific mechanism to trigger such action.

The Government considers that one option could be to strengthen the role of local councillors in this respect by giving them the right to trigger action on the part of police and other relevant agencies when they are presented with acute or persistent problems of crime or anti-social behaviour to which local communities have been unable to get an effective response. This would not be about individual complaints - nor could it be triggered by individuals - but rather by community groups, after persistent efforts to secure action have come to nothing. This power would give elected representatives greater ability to obtain a solution for their communities.

This new power would give communities a greater guarantee that they will be properly protected. But we recognise that it will be vital to put in place sufficient safeguards to prevent malicious or vexatious use of the power or its misuse by groups with extremist views. Councillors would have to demonstrate that the case met certain conditions before they were able to invoke the trigger power. Agencies would be able to decline requests under certain circumstances if, for example, they were frivolous, vexatious or would involve a disproportionate burden on agencies. We are proposing that this should be an avenue of last resort rather than a mainstream way of doing business.

Under this option, we think that local councillors should be able to trigger three levels of response on the part of the relevant agencies:

(i) obtaining information that was not being made available;

(ii) attendance by the relevant authority at a local public meeting;

(iii) action on the part of a wide range of specified agencies, including local councils, with a role to play in community safety.

In additon to proposals to strengthen the statutory responsibility of agencies to work together to tackle problems that require a multiagency solution, the trigger process would require a specific statutory duty - building on existing duties for partnership working under s.17 of the Crime and Disorder Act 1998 - to be placed on a wide range of other organisations, including other criminal justice agencies, to cooperate. Requests for action would be dealt with at the lowest appropriate level. We foresee that in many cases, this would begin with a meeting of all the relevant agencies and the local community to consider the problem and agree a course of action to resolve it. In doing so, all local agencies would be obliged to consider the full range of powers and interventions at their disposal.

The Government believes that the existence of the trigger mechanism will almost certainly mean a change in attitude and to practice which will make its use extremely infrequent. But we want to make sure that members of all communities -not just the well organised or vocal - can, in the final analysis, get action taken to deal with crime and anti-social behaviour in their neighbourhood. However, in advance of, and to inform the necessary legislation which would be required to put this trigger mechanism into effect, we will work through the practicalities of how it might operate, and we will do so with chief officers of police and others.

Above the neighbourhood level

Policing at the neighbourhood level cannot be looked at in isolation, or as somehow distinct from activity which takes place above this very local level. High performing, responsive neighbourhood policing must be supported by effective arrangements above this level - at what is commonly known as the Basic Command Unit (BCU) level within police forces. Effective partnership working at this level is vital since BCUs typically correspond to Crime and Disorder Reduction Partnership areas. The post of BCU Commander - usually held by a chief superintendent - is now one of the most important jobs in British policing.

The Government regards the leadership of BCU commanders to be crucial in terms of embedding a new customer service culture within forces and ensuring that neighbourhood policing is not simply some kind of bolt-on - rather it being mainstream activity.

Delegation to BCU Commanders

Delegation and devolution to the frontline is one of the Prime Minister's four principles of public service reform, essential in enabling true responsiveness to local needs and giving communities a greater say in the design and delivery of their local services.

The Government's 2001 policy paper on police reform 12 set out our commitment to exploring delegation and devolution in the policing context.

This was again highlighted in our November 2003 consultation paper Policing: Building Safer Communities Together to which respondents recognised the need to empower BCU commanders, with financial delegation seen by many as an essential part of this process.

The BCU fund was created during the 2002 Spending Review, as part of the Government's commitment to devolution and partnership working. £50m was assigned to the fund and distributed across forces nationally as ring-fenced funding. The intention was to give BCU Commanders considerable autonomy on how the money, delegated to them by the chief constable, was spent, with the one requirement that it should be used for funding local initiatives and must be agreed by CDRPs. The fund has been used successfully to tackle anti-social behaviour, to fund youth inclusion work, CCTV and drug prevention and in the provision of police support for such interventions. The feedback on the fund has been largely positive. The Government is committed to the continued funding of local initiatives and is looking at how the BCU fund should now be most effectively administered.

Additionally, the Police Standards Unit has undertaken preliminary research with a number of forces with the aim of identifying the key factors enabling BCU success. Not all BCU commanders have the same levels of financial freedom and the degree of delegation varies depending on the police force and its management culture. The issue of delegation is complex. Clearly, delegation - however it is executed - should not break the chain of command between a BCU commander and their chief officer.

The PSU's work has demonstrated that increased delegation to BCU commanders can increase their capacity to respond to local needs and can underpin sustainable performance improvements in the BCU and across the force. Delegation can increase the opportunities for creativity and innovation in operating practices at the local level. Importantly commanders who are able to make spending decisions themselves also feel able to play a more active and constructive role in partnerships.

However, the government recognises that delegation is not a panacea. Unless strong leadership, robust mechanisms of accountability and a clear operating framework are in place, poorly implemented or inappropriate delegation has the potential to undermine performance and destabilise a force. The challenge remains how to effectively "empower" BCU commanders while maintaining the coherence of the force and avoiding the creation of uneconomical units. The Government proposes to:

— carefully examine the precise role of BCU commanders and their contribution to partnership working. This will take into account the different contexts of policing across the country and address the balance of activities between those that are delegated and those that are better managed centrally; and

— develop further the key enablers of delegation to BCU Commanders. We will examine the importance of leadership, looking particularly at how far the direction and corporate vision which chief constables provide and the trust they exhibit in their commanders are essential for successful delegation to occur, and how this needs to be supported by appropriate training for all senior ranks. We will examine the use of stronger mechanisms for BCU commanders to be held accountable for their performance, and investigate the relationships between force HQs and BCUs, including how resources are to be balanced and negotiated between them to provide a clear operating framework.

5

Causes of Racial Disparity

Racial disparity in the criminal justice system exists when the proportion of a racial/ethnic group within the control of the system is greater than the proportion of such groups in the general population. The causes of such disparity may be varied and include differing levels of criminal activity, law enforcement emphasis on particular communities, legislative policies, and decision making by criminal justice practitioners who exercise broad discretion in the justice process.

Illegitimate or unwarranted racial disparity results from the dissimilar treatment by the criminal justice system of similarly situated people based on race. In some instances this may involve overt racial bias, while in others it may reflect the influence of factors that are only indirectly associated with race. There are four key aspects to addressing racial disparity in the criminal justice system:

1) The problem of racial disparity is one which builds at each stage of the criminal justice continuum of arrest through parole, rather than the result of the actions of any single agency.

2) In order to combat unwarranted disparity, strategies are required to tackle the problem at each stage of the criminal justice system, and to do so in a

coordinated way. Without a systemic approach to the problem, gains in one area may be offset by reversals in another.

3) Each decision point and component of the system requires unique strategies depending on the degree of disparity and the specific populations affected by the actions of that component.

Statistics from communities and the nation as a whole show evidence of the impact of racial disparity at all levels of the criminal justice system. These disparities often have a cumulative effect, whereby decisions made at one stage of the system contribute to increasing disparities at the following stages. For example, if bail practices result in similarly situated minorities being detained before trial at greater rates than whites, they will also be disadvantaged at trial and sentencing by having less access to defense counsel, community resources, and treatment options. Disparities in the system can be seen in the following:

— The widely-discussed phenomenon of "driving while black" illustrates the potential abuse of discretion by law enforcement. Traffic stops recorded on Interstate 95 in Maryland over a two year period revealed that African Americans represented 70 percent of drivers stopped and searched by police, while only 17.5% of all drivers - as well as speeders - were black.

— A New York state found that minorities charged with felonies were more likely to be detained than whites. The researchers concluded that 10 percent of minorities detained in New York City and 33 percent in other parts of the state would have been released prior to arraignment if minorities were detained at the rate of comparably situated whites.

— 46 percent of prison inmates and 42 percent of jail inmates are African American, compared to their 12 percent share of the overall population.

- — Hispanics constitute 18 percent of the prison population and 16 percent of the jail population, compared to their 12 percent share of the population.
- — A black male born in 1991 has a 29 percent chance of spending time in prison at some point in his life, a Hispanic male 16 percent, and a white male 4 percent. While the primary focus of this manual is on decision-making within the adult criminal justice system, the impacts of racial disparity are clearly seen in the juvenile justice system too. While African American youth represent 15% of their age group within the general population, they represent:
    - — 26% of juvenile arrests
    - — 31% of referrals to juvenile court
    - — 46% of waivers to adult court
    - — 58% of juveniles sentenced to adult prison

Racial disparity challenges the basic values upon which the criminal justice system rests. To the Systemwide change is impossible without informed criminal justice leaders who are willing and able to commit their personal and agency resources to measuring and addressing racial disparity at every stage of the criminal justice system, and as a result, for the system as a whole.

Addressing racial disparity in the criminal justice system is entirely consistent with a commitment to public safety and to a fair system of justice. If unwarranted racial disparities can be reduced, the justice system will gain credibility and serve a more effective role in preventing and responding to crime extent that such disparity is a result of racism (that is, discrimination based on race), it represents an outright rejection of the principle of equal justice. A commitment to values of justice, fairness and public safety compels professionals to vigorously address disparate treatment when and where it exists. A sense that the criminal justice system is fair is essential to the functioning of a democratic society. Thus, there must be a nexus between societal values and personal values: fairness and a commitment to due process is an absolute societal and personal dictum. Without this commitment, confidence in the rule of law erodes.

For example, since the police are the gatekeepers to the criminal justice system, fundamental mistrust and suspicion of police destroys the partnership between law enforcement and the community at the most direct contact point between the public and the system. Thus, pro-active approaches to building trust between law enforcement agencies and communities is essential.

Law enforcement and criminal justice agencies must publicly communicate their recognition of the fact that a racially imbalanced system will have a negative impact on families, communities and the larger society. In order for a democratic society to function effectively, communities must support law enforcement as an essential ingredient to good government. Law enforcement agencies must work in an organized and very public fashion to instill that trust.

Similarly, the willingness and commitment of citizens to understand and respect the sentencing process is highly dependent on a sense that the system reflects societal values. In recent years, the criminal justice system has often served as a focal point for community frustration about racial problems in the larger society. For this reason, it is vitally important that unwarranted racial disparities be addressed aggressively and publicly.

This chapter discusses the specific ways in which racial disparities may result from decision-making at various points in the criminal justice process, and suggests steps that can be taken by criminal justice practitioners to counter those effects. These decision-making points provide an opportunity for professionals to ensure that a person of color is treated fairly. It is important to recognize, however, that the criminal justice system operates within a larger social and political context that affects both its operation and the position of racial minorities as they come into that system.

Criminal justice professionals have the capacity to counter disparity in several ways: as citizens they can seek to influence the political process; as professionals within the system they can work together for systemic change; and as decisionmakers they can exercise discretion to offset the impact of racial disparity, whether it results from a larger social or political context or previous decisions within the system.

Thus, criminal justice professionals will find an awareness of the wider social context advantageous in developing strategies to ensure that their decisions within the system help reduce racial disparity. The wider social context and systemic causes of racial disparity include higher crime rates, inequitable resources, legislative decisions and overt bias:

Higher Crime Rates

Racial data for the commission of crime is unavailable as most crime is not reported and the perpetrators remain unknown. The most extensive statistics available are for the race of people arrested. Victimization calculation in which victims are asked to identify the perpetrators of crime are consistent with arrest data for many offenses. Arrest rates for some offenses suggest that African Americans are disproportionately involved in particular types of crime. For example, about 45% of arrests for violent crime and about 30% of arrests for property crime are of African Americans. However, when looking at arrest rates it is important to remember the context in which arrests are made.

Arrest rates are essentially an indicator of police activity in clearing crimes reported to them and crimes they observe themselves. Thus, they reflect the frequency with which crimes are reported, police decisions regarding offenses on which they will concentrate their attention and their resources, and the relative vulnerability of various crimes to arrest. Despite these limitations, crime statistics are consistently used as a measure of the degree of offending among different groups in the population.

Issues of both race and class impact the likelihood of involvement with the criminal justice system and treatment within the system. Poor people generally are over-represented at every stage of the criminal justice system and people of color are also disproportionately poor. Policing policies which take a zero-tolerance approach to minor violations of law have been disproportionately targeted at inner-city black and Hispanic populations. Policy and practice regarding plea negotiations and sentencing are shaped by public opinion, defendants' access to resources for effective defense, as well as their access to alternative means of treatment and problemsolving.

Therefore, the fact that official statistics consistently show poor and minority persons to be overrepresented among those arrested and convicted by the system must be tempered by the realization that these groups are the ones most lacking in the resources needed to avoid arrest and criminal justice punishment.

Further, individuals and communities with access to resources generally employ an approach to dealing with behavioral problems outside the juvenile and criminal justice systems. For example, middle class parents who have a child who is disruptive in school or engages in delinquent acts will explore the contributory role of learning disabilities, psychological problems or substance abuse with appropriate social service or health care professionals. They will engage private tutors, counseling and therapeutic services to remedy the problems they find. In the event of an arrest, they will typically deploy as many resources as possible as an alternative to further involvement in the juvenile or criminal justice systems.

The apparent overrepresentation of African Americans and other minorities involved in crime does not fully explain their overrepresentation in America's jails and prisons:

— In an examination of the overall racial composition of the 1991 state prison population, criminologist Alfred Blumstein concluded that 76% of the higher black rate of imprisonment could be accounted for by higher rates of arrest for serious offenses. The remaining 24% of disparity, Blumstein stated, might be explained by criminal histories and other factors such as racial bias.

— While these statistics held true for most crimes, the critical exception was drug offenses. African Americans constituted 15% of drug users in 1998, only slightly higher than their percentage in the population. However, African Americans represent 37% of those arrested for drug offenses, 53% of drug convictions, and 56% of drug offenders in prison.

— A related examination of incarceration data by leading sociologists found that while national level data seemed to show a high correlation between arrest rates and incarceration for African Americans, the variation in this relationship at the state level was quite significant. In the northeast states, only 69% of racial disparity in incarceration was explained by arrest, while in the north central states, fewer blacks were actually incarcerated than one would have predicted by just using arrest data.

Overall, these data suggest that a variety of factors, which include crime rates, law enforcement practices, and sentencing legislation, play a role in the degree of racial disparity in incarceration.

Another factor that may explain rates of incarceration is the criminal history of an offender. The more serious a prior criminal record, the greater the likelihood of receiving a prison term for a new offense. Whether one acquires a criminal record is clearly in part related to the level of criminal activity, but is also a function of race, geographic location and other factors. Disruptive and misbehaving youth from middle class neighborhoods have fewer arrests than similar youth from neighborhoods whose principal resources are the juvenile and criminal justice systems.

These factors may be compounded by law enforcement and criminal justice policies. For example, the disproportionate incidence of arrests of minority drivers for the "offense" of "driving while black" in recent years demonstrates the racial profiling through which members of minority groups may be more likely to enter the criminal justice system than similarly situated white drivers. This may result in a disproportionate number of blacks being arrested for non-violent drug crimes and acquiring a criminal record, as well as the sense of anger and humiliation which brought this practice to public attention.

A recent experiment of juvenile arrest, detention and incarceration rates found that, even adjusting for criminal history and seriousness of offense, minority youth were more likely that white youth to be detained, formally charged, transferred to criminal court and incarcerated. Having established a criminal record at an early age, both the likelihood of their future involvement in the system and the likelihood of receiving harsher punishments are increased. Another experiment has documented the complex interaction among several variables - race, sex, age and employment - in contributing to disparities.

If law enforcement resources are heavily focused in poor neighborhoods, if public safety strategy is limited to arrest and prosecution, if the indigenous organizations in the community are denied a voice in deciding how these problems should be addressed, and if there is seriously insufficient commitment of economic, educational and social service resources that might provide assistance and hope to the residents, this dimension of the racial disparity problem will simply grow worse.

Inequitable Access to Resources

Discussions of race and the criminal justice system are often heavily overlaid with considerations of class as well. Racial disparities are related in part to the volume of crime committed by various groups, but are also a function of differing forms of treatment that relate to the background and resources of the offender.

Analyses of youthful offending suggest that while criminal behavior cuts across race and class lines, the societal response to these behaviours may significantly influence the course of a potential criminal career. Decisions regarding the most effective balance of responses by law enforcement, social services, and community intervention are critical in determining many of the outcomes.

These often reflect broad policy decisions regarding economic investments in particular communities, provision of adequate educational and employment opportunities, and access to health care and treatment programs. The inequitable access to resources can result in very different outcomes for middle class and poor children with similar behavioral problems.

Once the decision has been made to rely on the criminal justice system as the primary response to social problems in poor minority communities, the day-today actions of practitioners are constrained by that decision. For example, police make more drug arrests in low-income neighborhoods because those communities are not provided with other options for dealing with drug problems. Within the criminal justice system the allocation of resources can have a compounding effect on defendants as they move through the system. This can manifest itself in some of the following ways:

— Bail and pretrial release screening instruments and release policies may have biases toward middle class values and resources - for example, an early release system that utilizes electronic monitoring which requires a telephone in the home will eliminate this pretrial release option for impoverished defendants.

— Prior to sentencing, resources necessary to treat addictions, consult with psychologists, or hire expert witnesses and investigators are often unavailable through public funding and so multiply the disadvantages for indigent defendants of any race. Public defenders with high caseloads may not be able to develop individualized alternative programs or sentencing options.

— A defendant who comes to court for sentencing directly from lock-up may be disheveled or angry, and viewed as a prisoner. Another defendant who has the resources to avoid pretrial detention will arrive well dressed and may be able to show a record of seeking treatment or other services prior to trial. These differences can lead to post-conviction disparities, where the "prisoner" remains in prison, and the "free" defendant remains free.

The Legislature

]Legislatures at the federal, state and local levels literally create the criminal justice system by passing laws that define prohibited behavior, the penalties to be imposed for violating those laws, and the processes by which cases are to be disposed and sentences are to be determined. Even county and city legislatures frequently pass local ordinances that are enforced by the police and the criminal courts.

Many of these laws have a disproportionate impact on minority communities, which could have been foreseen before the laws were passed. For example, by significantly increasing penalties for drug trafficking, especially for trafficking in crack cocaine, while lowering the weight of the drug required for charging felony possession with intent to sell, and mandating imprisonment for such a conviction, legislative drug policy has heavily affected minority communities. Moreover, given the nature of the crack versus cocaine marketing system, it should have been obvious that enforcement efforts would concentrate on the former rather than the latter, and that the crack markets were more visible and vulnerable in the neighborhoods of the minority poor.

Had these predictable effects been identified and considered by the legislatures, different responses to the drug problem might have been developed. Representatives of the communities most likely to be affected might have been actively engaged in thinking through a more comprehensive, less damaging, and more effective strategy for addressing the problem. More reasonable distinctions between minor and major drug offenses might have been enacted. A range of alternative responses to minor offenders, including drug treatment, might have been established. The discretion required to distinguish between dilettantes and professionals in the drug trade might have been left to the courts, which explore the actual circumstances of the offense and the histories of the offenders.

Public financing, committed in enormous amounts to policing and corrections, might have been made available in significant amounts for education, prevention, and treatment programs in the communities where the problem was most pronounced. The political furor over crime during the last fifteen years has driven legislatures to pass ever-more punitive laws resulting in enormous growth in prison and jail populations.

The vast majority of inmates are people of color, and as a whole they have been offered little in the way of training, education and meaningful drug treatment during periods of incarceration. This enormous increase in the use of jails and prisons has taken place without persuasive evidence indicating that incarcerative strategies are the only, or even the most effective, approach to controlling crime.

This suggests the need for legislatures to treat proposed criminal legislation with the same care many now accord to other legislation such as laws that will affect children's education or the environment. Thorough legislative impact analyses would identify probable disproportionate racial impacts and signal the need to seek alternative problem-solving strategies to eliminate or significantly lessen such effects. Indeed a requirement to perform such analyses would slow the legislative rush to simple punishment, provoke a more deliberative strategy development process, and encourage extensive and effective use of the range of public and private resources for assuring public safety.

Overt Bias

So long as racism exists within society at large, it will be found within the criminal justice system. Racism fuels the overt bias which can show in the language, attitude, conduct, assumptions, strategies and policies of criminal justice agencies. Instances of overt bias can lead in turn to the improper use of discretion which is at the core of much of the problem of racial disparity. Certainly, in the past two decades, much of the overt racist language and attitudes once common in many parts of the system are now considered out of bounds and have all but been eliminated in public settings.

However, out of the ear of the public, racism may still flourish behind the scenes. The need to address racism wherever it manifests itself is a key and basic component in reducing racial disparity. Bias in the criminal justice system may take many forms. In policing, it can manifest itself in police community interactions and the degree of respect and consideration that law enforcement displays to the public. In the courtroom, the way in which minority defendants or attorneys are addressed can communicate attitudes suggesting second-class status. Prison officials' interactions with families of inmates can also either aid in community-building or increase levels of resentment.

Criminal justice practitioners, like others, are likely to identify with those who look and act like them. Thus, judges and prosecutors may be more receptive to consideration of pretrial or sentencing options for defendants with whom they feel some connection. This is likely to hold true for all racial and ethnic groups. Understanding these dynamics reinforces the necessity to maintain a diverse and representative system of justice so as to more equitably meet the legitimate needs of all persons in the system.

Many observers suggest that overt bias in criminal justice decision-making has declined dramatically in the last couple of decades, and that racial disparity is essentially a consequence of policies, strategies, and decisions that unintentionally and indirectly produce disparate effects. While much of the research that has been conducted in the recent past tends to support that belief, racist attitudes persist among some people in all American institutions.

The U.S. Supreme Court recently set aside the death sentence in a Texas case in which the offender's Hispanic origin had been presented by the state as an indicator of likely "future dangerousness"-an aggravating factor pointing to death rather than life in prison as the appropriate punishment. An audit by the Texas attorney general's office found eight other cases that "may be similar" regarding testimony in capital punishment sentencing of blacks and Hispanics.

Guarding against such racist attitudes among criminal justice operatives is especially important, both because of the expectation that they must always act justly, and because they are so often called upon to exercise coercive authority over the citizenry. Therefore, there can be no relaxation of training in human relations, of orientations to the cultures and subcultures of the people with whom the criminal justice agents interact daily, and of supervisory oversight designed to detect and correct bias in the attitudes, speech, and behavior of subordinate personnel.

6

Racial Disparity at Decision Points in the Justice System

The criminal justice system can be seen as a process consisting of a series of points at which system personnel make decisions that result in introducing a person to the system, continuing or discharging that person from the system, and determining what will be done with the person while under supervision. Decision points range from police decisions regarding the enforcement of specific laws through parole decisions to terminate state supervision of an offender.

Virtually all of these decisions permit at least some discretion to the decision maker. The exercise of that discretion can produce racial disparity to the extent that the factors that influence the decision have a disproportionate impact on particular racial groups. It is neither desirable nor possible to eliminate discretion throughout the criminal justice system since much of the system is based on the judgment of the professionals involved in day-to-day decision making. What is needed is an introspective look at the substance of discretion and to find ways to either curb inappropriate uses, such as through the development of standards to guide its use, or to use discretion affirmatively to reduce racial disparity.

It is helpful, therefore, to identify the decision points where discretion is exercised, the system actors who participate at each stage, and the ways in which the decision may produce a disparate impact.

Enforcing the Law

The police are the first and most visible agents of the system. In addition to their general order maintenance functions, they are charged with responding to crime complaints, monitoring citizens' behavior in public places to discourage law violation, intervening with warnings, referrals, or arrests when such violations are suspected or observed, and assembling evidence for the prosecution of cases resulting in arrest.

These enormous responsibilities require the police to make strategic decisions about the kinds of offenses and offenders that will be given priority attention, and the distribution of police resources across neighborhoods, days of the week and time of the day. In addition, police agencies must make tactical decisions about how their resources will be deployed to implement the agency's priority objectives. The strategies and tactics for addressing those problems result in according greater attention to some problems than others, concentrating police resources in some neighborhoods rather than others, and employing more intrusive tactics in some areas than others.

Thus, the strategic and tactical decisions of the police often have a disproportionate impact on particular groups within their jurisdictions. There is a tendency to assume that the police are the sole participants in their own strategic and tactical decision-making. In fact, those decisions are subject to review and approval by the executive branch of government, including the office of the prosecutor, and frequently subject to positive or negative reactions from the legislative and judicial branches. In well-organized suburban communities, groups of residents and business people often work with the police in formulating these strategic and tactical decisions and reviewing their effects. This type of community involvement tends to be less evident in urban areas, especially in the neighborhoods of the poor.

However, in recent years, the advocates of community policing have insisted that such involvement should be the norm, and have worked with police agencies and community organizations to foster it. Especially in ethnically diverse areas, police officers are often working in areas that are culturally quite different from that with which they are familiar. Yet most training programs offer only general sessions on diversity and ethnic sensitivity. In the absence of a more specific orientation to the language, norms, values, traditions, and major institutions of the communities in which they work, officers will have difficulty understanding the needs and attitudes of the residents, and in communicating with them effectively.

Moreover, they are more likely to interpret the words and actions of people as insulting or rejecting of their authority, and they are more likely to speak and act in ways that are perceived as disrespectful by the people in the neighborhoods. These circumstances may adversely affect the officer's discretionary decision-making, and may lead to a sense of mutual alienation between the police and the community.

In the last several years, many departments have increased the use of "stop and frisk" tactics, especially in high crime areas. Regular patrol or special tactical officers will stop and question persons they perceive to be acting suspiciously, and often "pat down" the person for weapons. The tactic is intended to make the police presence felt in the area, and is believed to have a deterrent effect on conventional forms of street crime. In addition, the tactic does produce arrests for illegal weapons, outstanding warrants, and other offenses.

On the highways, road patrol officers often stop people for apparent traffic violations, and use the occasion to search the vehicle for drugs. These "pretext" stops have become a matter of considerable concern in several states based on the belief that people of color are grossly over-represented among those stopped. A State Attorney General in New Jersey has confirmed that suspicion, and set forth an elaborate plan for developing training for State Troopers in their use, the recording of data on all stops including the racial identity of the driver, the grounds for suspicion leading to the stop, and the action taken by the police officer pursuant to the stop. The plan also calls for regular monitoring of the database for evidence of disproportionate impact on various racial and ethnic groups.

In New York City, the extensive use of pedestrian stops has produced widespread complaints from residents of predominantly minority neighborhoods. These complaints led to an extensive investigation by the State's Attorney General, which discovered considerable statistical evidence of minority over-representation among those stopped, and anecdotal evidence of the intrusive and often insulting nature of these stops. The Attorney General's say committed to work with the Police Department and other interested parties to review, and modify if appropriate, the Department's guidelines for use by police officers in implementing such stops, and for police managers in monitoring their use.

Arraignment, Release, and Pre-Adjudicatory Decisions

Between the time a suspect is arrested and the time he or she is arraigned, a number of important activities take place where decisions are made that can have a dramatic effect on the racial composition of the criminal justice population. This critical stage in the processing of a criminal case is rendered more complicated because multiple players are involved, including: the police, the complainant, witnesses, the prosecutor, the suspect, the suspect's family and friends, the pretrial officer, the defense, diversion and alternative sanction programs, and the court. A reasonably careful review of the charges and the evidence by the police may result in a decision to void the arrest by declining to bring charges. Immediate consideration of the charges, evidence, and the arrest event by the prosecutor and the police helps to determine the decision to prosecute on specific charges, and to set parameters for plea negotiations.

In some jurisdictions, large proportions of misdemeanor cases are disposed and given nonincarcerative sentences at arraignment. The absence of a pretrial services program has often led to an assumption that bail should be set in all but capital cases, and that the bail amount should simply reflect the seriousness of the charge. Such assumptions discriminate against poor persons and result in unnecessarily high rates of detention. Detention, in turn, increases the likelihood of conviction and incarceration.

Early involvement of defense counsel facilitates the attorney's understanding of the case, counseling the client, and initiating as early as possible appropriate plea negotiations with the prosecution. A careful review of options at this point can result in a decision to defer prosecution on condition that the defendant participate successfully in a program of supervision and treatment. Alternatively, the case may be transferred to a special purpose court with sufficient resources to fashion a disposition and sentence that best imposes accountability, supervises behavior in the community, and provides meaningful opportunities for the defendant to change his or her lifestyle.

Adjudication and Sentencing

This stage of the criminal justice process begins with the continuance of a case beyond arraignment and ends with the disposition and imposition of sentence. Since the vast majority of criminal cases are disposed by plea, assuring that minorities are not disadvantaged in the process is critical. This assurance is just as important in the lower courts as it is in the higher trial courts.

Misdemeanor level crimes, which typically account for a majority of criminal cases, are brought to disposition and sentence in the lower courts. Although the sentences imposed in these courts are generally less severe than those imposed in the higher courts, a conviction becomes part of the defendant's criminal history and can lead to more severe treatment in subsequent cases. Moreover, because the cases are more numerous and the sentences less severe, less time and fewer resources are generally available for fashioning constructive, non-incarcerative sentences in the lower courts. Finally, attention to the lower court process is important because felony cases typically enter the system through arraignment and motion activity in the lower courts, and may be disposed there as well.

More serious cases, with a range of more severe penalties in the mix, are handled in the higher courts. The vast majority of these cases are also disposed by plea. Thus, it is crucial that the publicly supported defense bar, which usually represents the vast majority of poor, minority defendants, be accorded full and early discovery and be provided with adequate resources for investigators, expert witnesses, and the development of alternative sentencing plans. It is also essential that community-based service organizations, especially those serving minority communities, be available for use by the courts as components of community-based supervision and service programs, and that they be supported by public funds when providing such services.

Similarly, the probation service, which typically prepares pre-sentence say for consideration by the court, especially in felony cases, should have the training, resources and access to the defendant's community that are required to prepare multi-faceted sentencing proposals that respond effectively to offender need and accountability as well as public safety.

The experiment of probation presentence in juvenile court cases illustrates the means by which racial bias, whether intended or not, may influence sentencing outcomes. Researchers analyzing the narrative descriptions of juvenile offenders found that probation officers tended to portray the delinquency of black youth as stemming from negative attitudinal and personality traits, while the analysis of the behavior of white youth stressed the influence of the social environment. Black youth were judged to be more dangerous, which then translated into harsher sentences than for comparable white youth.

Finally, in recent years, special purpose courts have been developed to deal with issues such as drug cases, domestic violence cases, and other problems associated with the quality of life. These courts are based on the premise that concentrating the authority of the court on a specific problem enables that court to better hold offenders accountable for their behavior, and to compel their participation in treatment, restitution, community service, and skill development programs. They seek not only to adjudicate and punish, but also to compel activities that can solve or ameliorate the problem in the community and address the needs of the offender for skill development and drug treatment.

There is a concern that these courts will bring people into the criminal justice system whose problems would be better addressed outside it, and that they will consume resources that could be more effectively used in the community. However, once the decision to adjudicate a case in court has been made, it is important to assure that the factors used to determine a defendant's eligibility for transfer to these "specialty" courts do not inadvertently discriminate against racial minorities.

Probation and Community Supervision

While the number of jail and prison inmates has exploded in the last two decades, the number of offenders sentenced to probation has also grown dramatically. Persons of color, especially African- Americans, are disproportionately represented in both groups, but they are less likely than white offenders to receive a community corrections sentence. While part of the explanation for this may lie in an analysis of offense, convictions and criminal history, it may also be because the probation service and consequently the courts, are less familiar and less comfortable with the ethnic communities from which these defendants come. As a result, court officials may not recognize positive, neighborhood residents and resources in the defendant's life that could make constructive contributions to his supervision and treatment in the community.

This social and cultural distance between the probation service and the community may result in fewer recommendations for probation, or in supervision and sentencing plans that are less comprehensive and relevant to the defendant's life than they could be. In some jurisdictions, there are growing numbers of faith-based organizations and not-for-profit service organizations that are reaching out to the courts and to probation departments to serve as supervision and service agents for defendants given non-incarcerative sentences by the courts.

This is a trend that should be encouraged both to reduce the current level of reliance on incarceration for minority offenders, and to enhance their opportunities for adopting a law-abiding lifestyle. Thus, probation departments should be encouraged to decentralize their investigative and supervisory resources to the communities where probationers are concentrated, in order to increase their understanding of the local culture, and their interaction with local organizations and institutions. Such decentralization would also enable probation officials to assist the local service organizations to connect with the courts, to understand what is expected of them when participating in alternative sanction programs, and to develop the capacity to comply with those expectations. Violations of probation have contributed significantly to the increase in jail and prison populations.

When a violation is a consequence of committing a new and serious offense, incarceration is often mandatory. However, when the new offense is a non-violent, low-level misdemeanor, or when the violation is a consequence of the offender's inadequate compliance with the conditions of probation, the decision to return the case to court and to seek an incarcerative sentence is often discretionary on the part of the probation officials.

Thus, it is important that policies governing these discretionary decisions be put in place and reviewed to determine if and how they might have a disproportionate impact on minority offenders. Moreover, there is a critical need to develop a range of graduated sanctions which can be invoked by probation officers in response to non-compliant behavior by the probationer. In the absence of such a range, the probation official must choose between simply ignoring the behavior, which may be interpreted as accepting it, and returning the offender to court for re-sentencing.

Jail and Prison Custody

African American and Latino minorities comprise a dramatically disproportionate share of those in jail and prison. It is hoped that this situation will change in the years to come, and that the suggestions offered in this manual will help to bring that change about. While the removal of certain offenders from the community clearly has beneficial effects, there is increasing evidence of the damage experienced by minority communities when such a large percentage of their residents are incarcerated. Efforts must be made to reduce the violence, isolation, and boredom that typically characterize our jails and prisons, and to convert them into reasonably safe environments where inmates may receive the education, treatment, and skills training that will prepare them for lawabiding lives and employment upon their release.

The internal atmosphere in jails and prisons tends to be intense and often confrontational. The vast majority of the inmates are African Americans and Hispanics, while the vast majority of the correctional staff are white. Thus, there is often an undercurrent of racial and ethnic tension between the two groups. Similar strains can be found among inmates themselves, and sometimes produce conflicts and violence between race-based gangs within the institution. Prison and jail administrators need to be mindful of this factor, and strive to reduce racial tensions and prevent these inter-group hostilities from hardening into the grist of prison riots.

Inmates are deprived of regular contact with family and friends in the community, which has negative effects on both the community and the inmate. Families often encounter difficulties with respect to housing, finances, and child-rearing. Given their inability to help in such circumstances, inmates experience frustration and a loss of self-esteem. This, in turn, increases their volatility within the institution, and depresses their motivation to use what opportunities are available for treatment and skills development. This vicious cycle almost certainly contributes to the relatively high recidivism rates, especially within the first year of release.

The negative effects of isolation from the community can be eased substantially by establishing effective working relationships between the social services staff of the institution and the human service network in the community. This requires that there are community-based social service workers attached to the institution, and that the public and not-for-profit service agencies in the community are willing and able to take on this additional workload. It also requires that the institution provides opportunities for treatment and skills development. In the last few years, recognition of the need for institutional drug and alcohol treatment programs has been growing, but there is a continuing need to expand and improve them.

Moreover, treatment often ends when the inmate leaves the institution because arrangements have not been made for follow-up services in the community. As prison and jail populations have increased so sharply, the resources available for institutional education, counseling, and skills development programming have not kept up with the increased demand. Indeed, in some jurisdictions such programs have come to be defined as perks, which should not be provided to "undeserving" persons. Such deprivations intensify the problems of prison management, and return prisoners to the community even less equipped for effective and law-abiding lifestyles than when they were first imprisoned.

In recent years, the number of mentally ill, and mentally ill and chemically addicted (MICA) persons committed to jails and prisons has increased dramatically.

These inmates constitute a special challenge for correctional personnel, who often are not trained to understand their behavior and their needs. African American inmates tend to be "over diagnosed" in comparison with whites. African Americans tend to be diagnosed as schizophrenic proportionately more often than whites, while the latter tend to be diagnosed as presenting depressive symptoms. The differences in diagnosis may reflect the cultural distance between African American inmates and the generally white personnel in the psychological services positions, and may result in a different assessment of the potential "dangerousness" of the inmate.

In any case, the institutions are often significantly lacking in the resources needed to correctly diagnose and treat such people, and to connect them to community-based services upon release. Clearly mentally-ill inmates of all races need adequate services both in prison and back in the community; however, it appears that African Americans suffer most from the deficiencies in the current system.

Parole Decisions

There are three types of decisions made by parole authorities which bear significantly on the involvement of racial minorities in the criminal justice system. In those states which still use indeterminate sentencing systems, parole authorities decide when offenders will be released from prison to the community. Secondly, these authorities make decisions about the release plan which the offender must follow when he returns to the community. Finally, parole officers monitor the parolee's compliance with those conditions, decide when to violate someone for non-compliance, and pass such cases to the parole commission for a decision on appropriate sanctions, including return to prison.

7

Understanding Racial Disparity

The evidence may point to a relatively low degree of disparity in some jurisdictions, while in other jurisdictions the need for studied approaches to reduce disparity are apparent. The following framework outlines a means by which jurisdictions can begin a five step process to address this issue by:

1) Determining whether the percentage of people of color involved at any stage of the criminal justice system is disproportionate
2) Identifying the reasons for any disparity identified and the extent to which it is legitimate
3) Assessing the decision points where disproportionate disparities may occur
4) Designing and implementing strategies to reduce disparities
5) Monitoring the effectiveness of the strategies.

Identify Disproportionate Representation

Complete a matrix to determine if criminal justice

processing at any stage of the system is disproportionate. Developing such a matrix first involves computing the proportion of persons of color involved at each stage of the criminal justice process (e.g., arrest, pretrial confinement, conviction, incarceration) and then comparing these proportions with the percentage of people of color in the population, and with the percentage of people of color at the preceding stage of the disposition process.

In constructing this type of matrix to shed light on the issue of over-representation, the base population used may be different from the general population figures used in the illustration. Forexample, if the focus of attention is on the juvenile justice system, it would be more appropriate to use as a base the at-risk population of juveniles between 10 and 17.

Alternatively, instead of using general population statistics as a base for both juvenile and adult arrests, one might use a base of persons between the ages of 10 and 35, the crime-prone years. In some communities, if the data are available, it would be helpful to complete a separate matrix for each of the groups - African American, Latinos, Native Americans - included in the single "minority" group in this example.

In other versions of this matrix, the Disparity Index may be calculated by comparing the relationship between the percentage of minorities at each stage and their percentage in the total population under consideration. While this provides a good overview of the cumulative disparities throughout the system, it is less helpful in analyzing the specific impact of decisions made at each point within the system which are the focus of this manual.

Identify Reasons for Disparity

The matrix will identify the decision points at which disparity exists and estimate the extent of that disparity. The next step is to attempt to identify possible reasons for the various points of disparity. This exploration must include factors that are appropriate influences in the decisions such as the seriousness of the offense, the nature of the defendant's criminal history, and the nature and effects of prior criminal sanctions.

To the extent that the data on these factors are quantifiable, statistical regression techniques can be used to control for their influence. To the extent that disparity of outcomes persist, even after the legitimate factors are taken into account, its roots should be searched for in other areas of policy and discretion.

Assess Decision Points

Assess the decision points where discretion, policy choices, or resource allocation may contribute to over representation. This can be accomplished by "unpacking" the decision point into the prior decisions that produce it, and assessing the extent to which each of those decisions may have a negative and disproportionate impact on minority defendants. For example, if poor people are not represented by a competent publicly-supported attorney at the appearance at which bail is set, fewer of them may be released on their own recognizance, and the bails set may be higher than they would have been had the defendants been represented. Thus, poor people will be more likely to be detained for failure to post bail.

Exploring the effects of policies and discretionary decision-making may be accomplished by a variety of qualitative techniques including observation of practitioners at work, interviewing them, or bringing several of them together in focus groups to discuss the decisions they make and how they make them. When this effort reveals the influence of a factor which impacts disproportionately on minority defendants, the group of practitioners can then reconsider whether that factor is crucial to the decision, or whether its negative influence can be countered by some alternate form of community supervision.

DESIGN AND IMPLEMENT STRATEGIES

Design and implement strategies to reduce over representation by focusing on the decision points and the discretion or agency policy which may be related to the disparate results. The previous section of this manual looked at the potentially disparate impact of actions and policy at these decision points. The following section will discuss the design and implementation of strategies to reduce disparities.

MONITOR EFFECTIVENESS

Monitor the interventions on a regular basis to determine what is and is not working to reduce disparity. Moreover, regular monitoring is likely to identify influences and potential responses to them that were not recognized initially. In this way, progress can be made incrementally. In seeking to identify and correct the sources of racial disparity, it is important to remember that systemic change can only be effective if it is implemented throughout the system.

Since there will be turnover at the top levels of agency management, it is important that attention to issues of disparity take place at all levels of an organization. While deep-seated beliefs are difficult to change, professional behavior can be changed, beginning with a "zero tolerance" policy for overt bias. Overt bias is less likely to manifest itself as long as lines of communication are open. Personalrelationships break down stereotypes within agencies and between agencies and communities. Having people of color in leadership and decision-making positions can aid in challenging attitudes and stereotypes. This will often result in a gradual impact on institutionalized attitudes.

8

Options for Reducing Racial Disparity

For each of the major components of the criminal justice system, a series of options are offered for local consideration on how to reduce racial disparity. Following a listing of the options, a general discussion is included to aid the reader in understanding more clearly how some of the options may reduce disparity and why they are important.

Law Enforcement

— Undertake a research process similar to that described earlier in this manual to determine if members of minority groups are disproportionately represented at key police decision points, including:

  — traffic stops

  — pedestrian stops and frisks

  — arrests

  — access to alternatives to arrest.

At each point at which such disproportionate representation is evident, initiate a process with department managers and line staff, as well as representatives of minority communities, to examine policies, guidelines, and practices in terms of the contribution they may make to such disproportionality, and to develop effective corrective measures.

Development of Community Policing Approaches

— Initiate a process of transforming the department to a community policing model of service.

— Toward that end, create structures and processes, especially in high crime neighborhoods, designed to encourage the participation of community leaders and residents in defining the major concerns of the community and in designing and implementing problem-solving strategies to address them.

— Use these neighborhood structures and public forums to anticipate racially and ethnically disparate impacts from proposed problem-solving strategies and tactics.

— Institute public feedback forums to sensitize both the public and the police to cultural and racial issues, and to provide opportunities for discussion. From the law enforcement agency perspective, design a "human relations approach" by using Police Advisory Boards to open lines of communication to public; from the public's perspective, assess how law enforcement strategies are developed to assure that they are the result of an assessment of constructive approaches.

Monitor and Record Data on Traffic and Pedestrian Stops

— Institute concrete measures to monitor and record information regarding traffic and pedestrian stops to ensure that race is not a factor in the decision to stop. These should include recording all stops in terms of the identity of the person stopped, including race/

ethnicity, the date, the time and place of the stop, the reason for the stop, the police officer's observations that led to the stop, and the outcome of the stop.

— Provide persons who are stopped with written information regarding individual rights and process for filing complaints.

Develop Alternatives to Arrest

— Encourage service and faith-based organizations in minority communities to develop service programs that may be used by police officers and supervisors as alternatives to arrest and detention in cases in which the police have such discretion. Develop guidelines to help the officers use these alternatives fairly and effectively.

— Engage communities in development of problem-solving responses to local problems, particularly in regard to drug abuse.

Operations and Training

— Develop special orientation training for police personnel working in precincts, or neighborhoods, which contain substantial numbers of minority group members. These sessions should introduce the police to the residents, organizations, and cultural characteristics of the neighborhoods, so as to enhance their understanding of the symbols of respect in that neighborhood, and sharpen their ability to distinguish between activities and conditions that are and are not problematic in that community.

— Develop "early warning" systems to identify officers for whom excessive complaints regarding use of force or misconduct have been filed and initiate remedial action when necessary.

— Focus the attention of supervisors and managers on issues of racial disparity. Teach them to use the departmental database to monitor for instances of apparently racially disparate treatment by their subordinates, and investigate the reasons for such. Make certain that acts of racially disparate treatment are prohibited by and responded to within the department's disciplinary system.

— Ensure that persons promoted into supervisory and managerial positions are sensitive to and educated about issues related to race and race relations.

— Implement personnel evaluation and training programs designed to expand the number of minority group members among the department's management teams.

Undertake Public Education Regarding Approaches to Racial Disparity

— Launch public campaigns, in conjunction with representatives of minority communities, to educate the public and members of the department on the importance of racial sensitivity and fairness in law enforcement and criminal justice, to describe what the department is doing in that regard, and the successes that have been achieved.

— Use the department's budget requests and presentations to highlight the funds needed for and committed to initiatives related to racial fairness and sensitivity, and to insure legislative support for these goals and objectives.

Insufficient funding for law enforcement agencies can hinder progress in reducing racial disparity. Adequate attention - which starts with leadership but requires funding - to training, research, investigation and the allocation of officers for community policing, must be provided over time in order to most effectively respond to racial disparity. For example, without fully funded options for law enforcement to use as an alternative to arrest for low level public disorder crimes such as public drunkenness and crimes associated with homelessness, officers on the street have no choice but to arrest or ignore the crime. Options must be in place for discretion to be most productive.

People in low-income minority communities often evince considerable ambivalence on the question of whether they have too little or too much experience with police resources. Whatever the volume of resources committed to a community might be, the critical issue to the residents and organizations is access to opportunities to influence police decision-making and operations.

Minority residents will believe that they are better served, and less frequently abused, by police services to the extent that they are involved in the identification of priority problems in the community; in the formulation of strategies and tactics by the police and other relevant agencies to address those problems, in the decision to deploy the resources of the police and other relevant agencies; and in the process of monitoring and assessing the effects of the problem-solving strategies attempted. These collective desires are consistent with the principles of community policing, and should be advocated for by leadership in law enforcement. However, there is much to be learned about how the structures and processes for such integral engagement with the community can be constructed and sustained.

Cultural acclimatization can be part of the effort to strengthen the bonds between the police and the community. In each precinct, or community where minorities are prominently represented, cultural familiarity programs can be constructed for all police personnel serving that area. Such programs should be designed and implemented with representatives of the community to: introduce the officers to friendly local faces; orient them to the language, culture and traditions of the community; introduce them to representatives of local institutions that can assist them in their work; identify the kinds of problems about which residents are most concerned, and the kinds of police tactics that are considered unnecessarily intrusive; explain to them styles of speech and interaction that are considered respectful and those which are considered insulting. Such orientations can be valuable to police officials who are otherwise exercising discretion in an unfamiliar context, where they do not know the people, the place or the culture.

They can also help to reduce the officers' sense of distance from the community and their belief that the residents look on them with hostility, as shown in Vera's research on community policing in New York. Perhaps more than in any other agency, police conduct follows policy and strategy; in other words, agency policy, or lack thereof, dictates how line officers are expected to act in given situations. Therefore, policy decisions made by law enforcement can be expected to have an effect on line officers in daily contacts with the public. In regard to drug policy, for example, a decision made to focus police attention on street-corner drug use and sales could have differing impacts. It could be viewed by a community as support in combating a neighborhood problem, or as a hostile move aimed at removing young men and women from the community. Likewise, police officers might view the community as either one besieged by a handful of criminals or as a drug-infested "problem." The best check against ill-formed policy, strategy or tactics is for police officials to develop and review them in concert with representatives of the communities in which they will be implemented.

Police use of discretion has received much attention in recent years on the issue of "racial profiling" in traffic and pedestrian stops. Efforts to address the problem of racial profiling can begin with documentation of the problem through data collection. Police officials in San Diego and New Jersey, for example, now require the race and ethnicity of all persons stopped by the police to be\ recorded, along with other information that is routinely collected, and the President has directed all federal law enforcement agencies to collect data of this kind. These data will help to determine whether, where, and when stopping practices are disparate and thereby point to practice that needs correction. Moreover, they can help identify areas where modification in policies, guidelines and training is needed.

The Bureau of Justice Assistance argue that as of mid-year 1999, ten of the nation's 49 state law enforcement agencies whose primary duties include highway patrol required officers to record demographic information on the driver or passengers of all traffic stops. Thirty two State agencies say that specifically collecting racial or ethnic data on drivers who receive traffic-related citations. At least one jurisdiction has implemented a practice that at certain types of traffic stops a brochure is provided that describes the individual's rights and indicates who the individual would address a complaints to, as well as the officer's business card.

Leadership and supervision are key - including second-tier supervisors overseeing behaviour on the street. The line supervisor's role is crucial as guide and coach and supervisors need to be prepared and trained for their role. Field training officer status should only go to experienced and demonstrably "good" officers. The training officer should have high status and be held accountable for the behaviour of his/her subordinates.

Police agencies can introduce early warning systems - a certain number of complaints about use of force or other misconduct would trigger an initial internal investigation. Aggregate individual statistics feed into unit behaviour statistics and lead to individual and unit accountability. Indeed, accountability systems for police managers have been receiving a great deal of attention lately driven by the success of the COMPSTAT system in New York City. Such systems should be required to track patterns of racial disparity and civilian complaints. When police commanders are required to answer for their subordinates' sins of omission or commission, they will concentrate on correcting them.

Pretrial

— Undertake a research process similar to that described earlier in this manual to determine if members of minority groups are disproportionately represented among those who are:

  — denied release on recognizance or supervised release

  — subjected to bail amounts which they cannot post;

  — denied admission to diversion

  — deferred prosecution, or alternative sanction programs at this point in the process

  — detained because of their inability to post bail.

— If such disproportion is evident, initiate a process with front-end decision makers (police, pretrial, prosecution, defense, and court officials), as well as representatives of minority communities, to examine policies, guidelines, and practices in terms of the contribution they may currently make to such disproportionality, and to develop effective corrective measures.

Education and Advocacy

— Make certain that all participants in the pretrial process understand and agree that: the defendant is presumed innocent; he or she is entitled to pretrial release under the least restrictive alternative available; conditions of release, including bail, should be imposed only to reduce the risk of the defendant's failing to return to court (flight), or to reduce the risk to public safety, or both.

— Make certain that a pretrial service capable of assessing the risks of defendant flight, and (as required in some but not all jurisdictions) the risk of public safety posed by release, is available to all defendants after arrest and, if possible, before the arraignment.

— Reach agreement within the jurisdiction about the importance of the early release decision because it will profoundly affect the outcome of the case, and because it is one of the earliest points in the system where significant and important information about the offender is gathered that can be used to make fair and objective evaluations about offender characteristics and risk which are not driven by race, ethnicity, gender or class.

— Make training in pretrial decision making available to all criminal justice officials involved in making or influencing such decisions, including judges, prosecutors, defense counsel, and pretrial program directors, and other human services providers.

— Develop strong bonds with other criminal justice agencies and personnel and with community and advocacy groups for collaboration on public education about the early release decision and issues related to early release.

— Assure that the due process rights of all defendants, including the confidentiality of information voluntarily provided prior to adjudication, are protected in the process of deciding on casediversion, deferred prosecution, or alternative sanction programs following a negotiated plea at this point in the process.

— Assure the participation of community resources such as faith-based institutions and social service programs in developing defendant services that can be used as conditions of release, case diversion, or sentencing alternatives at this point in the process.

Institute Race-Neutral Policies and Procedures

— Develop exemplary protocols for all pretrial decisions using the standards developed by the National Association of Pretrial Agencies (NAPSA) that will reduce the potential for disparity.

— Review interview forms, risk assessment instruments and the recommended options to assure that none discriminate against poor people or minorities and, if they do, to establish alternative means to assure equal treatment.

— When performing the pretrial task of Information Gathering, reduce the propensity for racial disparity by instituting policies and procedures which:

  — Include all defendants held in custody pending disposition.

  — Prior to the interview, provide the detainee with information about the pretrial interview and release options.

  — Time the interview prior to initial appearance as a source of information for the bail/release decision.

— During the interview determine, in addition to the presence of drug use, treatment involvement and other indications of attempts by the defendant to discontinue drug use such as counseling, AA, etc.

— During the records check, distinguish between categories of offenses, i.e. felony vs. misdemeanor, convictions vs. arrests; violent crimes vs. non-violent crimes.

— During verification procedures, use extended family and other social contacts (for example, church and other association contacts), in addition to conventional references. Ask for input from defense counsel on these contacts.

When instituting Release Assessment Procedures, include in the design:

— An assessment scheme which can check for factors such as employment, residence, and prior record when determining the level of offender risk to the community and the risk of not returning to court (flight). Determine acceptable levels of over-rides to assessment approaches (such as point systems), and provide training on reasons for over-ride. (While an assessment of case strength may be germane to estimating the risk of flight posed by the defendant, it can only be the responsibility of the court, and not the pretrial officer.)

— An array of release options that includes non-traditional or non-conventional options such as custody to a church group or a member of the extended family, the use of electronic monitoring, etc.

— A pretrial report presentation in written form with a staff person assigned to the court for any needed further explanations. This requires significant planning and continual training.

— Well-enforced confidentiality standards.

— Supervisory oversight on consistency of assessment schemes.

— When performing Supervision and Follow-Up Functions, respond to the following issues:

  — A supervision plan developed with significant contact with other agencies for referral, the development of a written, individualized plan, written standards and violation procedures.

  — Follow up court notification which includes non-conventional means of contact including the use of a pager or contact through a relative.

  — During location and return of defendants who fail to appear, obtain proper references to check to validate reasons for non-appearance, e.g., due to hospitalization, etc.

  — During the regular review of the pretrial population, check to see if defendants' circumstances have changed as part of a systematic review process.

— Make certain that Management Information Systems:

  — Have a long- term value in the specific data elements that are collected so that the MIS can generate meaningful matter on a regular basis.

  — Keep complete and meticulous records of defendants who are interviewed, released, monitored, etc. The information should be used to enhance the process of obtaining and assessing information that is important for bail decisions.

  — Include race as one of the defendant-based data elements so that issues of racial disparity can be monitored regularly.

— Examine the data to assess whether the defendant population base is changing and whether the resource needs and availability may therefore be changing.

Reaching agreement within the justice system about the importance of the early release decision is one of the most critical steps a jurisdiction can take to reduce racial disparity. The pre-trial release decision is one of the earliest points in the system where significant and important information about the defendant is gathered that can be used to make fair and objective evaluations about defendant characteristics and risk which are not driven by race, ethnicity, gender or class.

The key stakeholders in the criminal justice system and the general public need to know that the only goals of the bail decision are to ensure that the defendant makes all court appearances and to reduce the risk of danger to the community that the defendant may pose if released pending case disposition.

Bail is not intended to punish a person who is not yet convicted. Bail is not intended to hold a person who is of no or little risk to flee the jurisdiction of the court or to reoffend while released. Educational messages need to make it clear that decisions of release are founded upon the fundamental right of due process, without prejudice against race, ethnicity, gender, or class. This is already stated in the Federal and state constitutions and in the release statutes. It should also be a part of the mission statement of every pretrial services agency.

Education should be provided to all criminal justice officials, the community, and the media. Pretrial programs should not wait for a notorious case, one typically involving a person released pretrial who allegedly commits a heinous crime, to become a focus of attention. Pretrial programs should make regular statistical matter available to the public. New programs, such as mental health screening, drug and alcohol treatment referrals, should be announced.

Pretrial agencies need to develop strong bonds with other criminal justice agencies and personnel especially law enforcement-and with community and advocacy groups in order to collaborate on public education about the early release decision and issues related to early release: the importance of offender assessment; the problem of jail crowding; the goals of pretrial release and bail.

An important first step to eliminate the unfairness of the bail system is to disassociate it from financial resources. The American Bar Association, National District Attorneys Association and National Association of Pretrial Services Agencies (NAPSA) all advocate the elimination of commercial bail bonding; NAPSA goes further by also advocating the elimination of all financial bail. This would certainly bring about a more equitable system of pretrial release because the conditions would not be related to a person's financial resources but rather to the risk that the person represents.

A second step is to assure that the mechanism used to assess risk is devoid of any discriminatory factors. Specifically, ascertain that people without permanent employment, or home, or owners of a telephone are not automatically considered higher risks than people with those attributes and possessions. A third step is to use agency databases to assure that the non-financial conditions of release that are imposed do not discriminate on the basis of race, ethnicity, gender, religion or economic means.

Pretrial programs should also recruit persons of color and diverse ethnic backgrounds. Defendants may be more likely to cooperate with such individuals. The instruments that they use and waivers they read to defendants should be in the language that the defendant understands.

Prosecution

Research and Assessment of Disparity

— Undertake a research process similar to that described earlier in this manual to determine if minority defendants are treated disparately by assistant prosecutors in terms of:

  — the bail/release request

  — charging decisions

  — access to diversion programs

  — approvals for deferred prosecution

  — plea offers and sentence requests

  — access to alternative sanction programs.

— If such disparity is evident, initiate a review of the office's policies and practices to identify ways in which they may inadvertently produce racially disparate results, and to develop appropriate corrective measures.

— Collaborate with other system actors and representatives of minority communities to identify racially disparate criminal justice outcomes, determine the reasons for them, and develop appropriate corrective measures.

— Examine role of race in capital cases from both the perspective of the accused and from the perspective of the assigned counsel. Are capital cases represented by the least prepared and experienced attorneys? Does the race of victim or defendant appear to influence the charging decisions in capital cases? Monitor any unwarranted racial disparities and determine ways to reform the system accordingly.

Neighborhood Problem-solving Strategies

— Identify neighborhoods that produce a disproportionate caseload for the office, and participate in collaborative efforts with other system actors and representatives of minority communities to develop effective strategies for solving the problems that produce the arrests, and to create and support alternative services for appropriate referrals of cases at various points in the disposition process.

— Examine the impact on specific neighborhoods of "get tough" drug policies such as mandatory minimums. What is the basis for such policies? Do these laws have a disparate effect in neighborhoods of color? If so, what is the human side of the statistics? What alternative policies can address the problem of drug abuse while reducing racial disparities?

Develop and Monitor Prosecutorial Guidelines

— Institute workable guidelines for charging, discovery, bail/release requests, plea bargaining and prosecutorial diversion which are race, class and gender sensitive. Utilize American Bar Association and National District Attorney Association standards as a starting point. Such guidelines can help protect the discretionary power of the prosecutor's office. Since standards that are deemed to be race neutral on the surface may in fact produce racially disparate outcomes, these need to be monitored and evaluated on an ongoing basis.

— Examine how administrative practices may need to be modified to avoid disparity: difficulties in communication with victims because they lack telephones or are hard to contact at work or home; language barriers; victims with inflexible work schedules who are unable to attend court appearances, etc.

Engage in Public Advocacy Regarding Disparities

— Take public or private positions against legislation which has historically resulted in disparate treatment of minorities.

— Support the development of standards in other criminal justice agencies for pretrial release and bail.

— Urge the adoption in Continuing Education Programs of curricula around the issues of race relations and the causes and effects of racial disparity.

Encourage Diversity in the Legal Profession

— Take an active role in the recruitment and advancement of attorneys in the local Bar Association who will focus attention on the problem of racial disparity in the criminal justice system.

— Work with local law schools to determine status of minority representation among student body and work to achieve effective affirmative action policies to encourage the recruitment of minority students.

— Work with local law schools to encourage inclusion in Juris Doctor program curricula that sensitize aspiring attorneys to the issues of race and racial disparity.

Prosecutors generally have very significant discretion - often statutorily based - which can have a tremendous impact on racial disparity. For example, prosecutors choose whether and what to charge, and their decisions are largely not subject to challenge. As with all discretion, this power holds the potential both for appropriate individualized decision making and for abuse.

One of the most illustrative examples of this discretion is in the area of bail recommendations, where prosecutors exercise broad discretion. Bail decisions - especially in urban centers - are often treated rather automatically; i.e., it is generally assumed that some amount of bail should be demanded in all criminal cases, and the more serious the charge, the higher the bail should be. Policies based on these assumptions invariably hurt poor defendants.

The prosecutor's primary purposes at this stage of the criminal justice process are to:

1) determine the best way to encourage the offender to return to court; and,

2) to protect the community from offenses which the defendant may commit while on release.

These purposes may not always be clearly thought through on a case by case basis.

Moreover, the efficacy of bail, as compared with other forms of release, in achieving those purposes may not be fully considered. And the use of higher bails intended to detain the defendant may actually be used to force a plea, a purpose that can only be described as "extralegal." Together, these practices likely will result in detaining many more defendants than is necessary, either in the interests of assuring appearance or in the protection of public safety. Since pretrial detention is highly predictive of post-conviction incarceration, prosecutors must make certain that the bail recommendation is arrived at after careful consideration of a range of release mechanisms to achieve the two purposes of bail. Thus, prosecutors should work with other system actors and community representatives to develop bail/release guidelines that are effective, efficient, and consistent with those purposes.

Policies that encourage full and early discovery for the defense are also important. They may facilitate earlier release of detainees, as well as early exploration of deferred prosecution and nonincarcerative sentencing alternatives. In that minority defendants constitute such a high proportion of those whose cases are processed by the system, they are the most likely beneficiaries of such policies.

While the discretion exercised by prosecutors in individual cases is appropriate and not a function expected to be decided in the public arena, the policies which shape the exercise of that discretion should be open to public input and even periodic review. Toward that end, some prosecution offices are attempting to create meaningful liaisons with local communities both to enhance their understanding of the community's concerns and ways in which the prosecution office can address them, and to enhance the public's understanding of how prosecutors' offices operate. This kind of "community prosecution" may also expand the prosecutor's knowledge and use of local programs that can serve as diversion or alternative sanction mechanisms.

If prosecutors at high levels take a leadership role to advocate change in the way that prosecutorial discretion is used, this may forestall legislative initiatives - such as the institution of prosecutorial guidelines which curb discretion - which may conflict with prosecutors' practical needs. Prosecutors are thus encouraged to call for and participate in research that provides insight into the impact of prosecutorial discretion, particularly in the area of racial disparity. In some jurisdictions, other agencies such as the judiciary track information relative to the use of discretion of the prosecutor's office. This practice should be encouraged by prosecutors and should be jointly developed in a collaborative spirit.

To monitor the exercise and effects of prosecutorial discretion, prosecutors should collect racial data on bail/ release requests, charging, and plea bargaining to make the process more transparent. They can also document decisions of their staff regarding mandatory sentencing - whether they seek the full punishment of the law or reduce or withdraw charges, and if so, to determine the rationale for their decisions. States that have Three Strikes legislation are particularly important sites for such examinations.

The charging decision represents one of the most critical stages of the criminal justice system, with considerable potential for reducing or expanding racial disparity. For example, ostensibly raceneutral standards that consider the "interest of victims in prosecution" as a charging criterion may work against the interests of minority victims. If such victims do not have a telephone at home or a work schedule that is flexible enough to permit time off for meetings with prosecutors or to appear in court, they may appear to some prosecutors to be "less interested" in the case. Or, a standard that considers the "likelihood of conviction" as a criterion may lead to racial biases as well. If, as has been shown in capital cases and some felony studies, cases of black offenders and white victims are more likely to lead to conviction than other victim-offender combinations, then the charging decision may in fact reinforce such biases.

Prosecutors and their staff need to examine the type of discretion available to them with respect to new "specialty courts" such as drug courts, domestic violence courts, and weapons courts to determine what is chargeable and what is divertable, how decisions are made, and whether there is any inappropriate racial impact.

Prosecutors may find it useful to bring together all criminal justice agencies to collaborate on racial disparity issues for periodic meetings regarding system fairness and effectiveness and use these meetings as a forum to discuss internal reforms as well as motivate other agencies to take similar steps. These meetings would include public defenders, the private bar, prosecutorial staff including special prosecution units, police, judges, and victims.

Public education efforts are required because, as elected officials, prosecutors must make their policies and practices understandable to the general public. Visibility and transparency are key to good government, suggesting that prosecutors seek opportunities to meet with citizens to talk about costs, alternatives, programming successes, and the rationale for addressing racial disparities.

Defense

— The defense bar, using its own or some other component's research, must identify those points in the case disposition process at which racial disparity is evident, explore how the policies, practices, and allocation of resources for the defense may contribute to that disparity, and advocate for appropriate corrective measures.

Effective Representation

— The defense bar must advocate for, and the system must provide for, effective representation as soon as possible after arrest.

— The defense bar must advocate for, and the system must provide for, access to appropriate diagnostic and assessment services at an early stage of representation.

— The defense bar should advocate for full discovery as soon after the arrest as evidence is produced by the prosecution, in order to prepare an effective defense, including an individualized sentencing proposal in felony cases.

— When client and/or offense present cultural issues unfamiliar to the defense attorney, build a team of family, community and other professionals from that culture to increase understanding of the dynamics of the case.

— Develop directories of area service and community organizations for use by local attorneys.

— Educate local defense attorneys on the existence of programs and special courts so that they can form a judgment regarding the role of such courts in providing services and the potential for reducing disparity.

— Provide opportunities for defense counsel training to improve competency for defense of youthful offenders (such as the ABA National Juvenile Defender Center) and in the use of psychological research for effective defense.

— Examine the role of race in capital cases from both the perspective of the accused and from the perspective of the assigned counsel; are capital cases represented by the least prepared and experienced attorneys? Are the resources adequate for effective defense in such cases?

Advocate for Appropriate Pretrial Release Services

— The defense bar should advocate for the provision of pretrial services for all defendants held in custody as soon as possible after the arrest.

— The defense bar should insist that bail/release requests made by the prosecutor, and bail/release decisions made by the court, be justified only in terms of the defendant's risk of flight, or risk to public safety upon release, or both, and the absence of any less intrusive alternative for reducing that risk.

Sentencing Advocacy

— Defense attorneys should utilize sentencing advocates who can develop sentencing proposals for the court in felony cases and jointly challenge unwarranted disparities at sentencing.

— Public defense offices should establish effective working relationships with the schools, faithbased organizations, and social service organizations operating in communities in which a significant portion of criminal defendants reside in order to enhance their ability to prepare such sentencing plans, to advocate for their use by the court, and to monitor their effective implementation.

Legal Education and Advocacy

— Utilize the local Bar Association and Criminal Defense Attorney Association to become active on the issue of racial disparity: educate, analyze and improve the way defense attorneys understand and deal with the problems of racial disparity.

— Organize the Bar Association and/or the local Criminal Defense Attorney Association to call for standards and guidelines for bail, pretrial release, prosecutorial diversion, charge and plea bargaining.

— Organize the Bar Association and/or the local Criminal Defense Attorney Association to call for the development and funding of specific efforts to reduce minority representation at all stages of the justice process.

— Take an active role in the recruitment and advancement of attorneys in the local Bar Association who will focus attention on issues of racial disparity in the criminal justice system.

— Work with local law schools to determine status of minority representation among student body and work to achieve effective affirmative action policies to encourage the recruitment of minority students.

— Work with local law schools to encourage inclusion in Juris Doctor program curricula which sensitizes aspiring attorneys to the issues of race and racial disparity.

— Provide to local law schools the opportunity for practicums involving hands-on court room and client based work to offer more experience to the school program.

— Urge the adoption in Continuing Education Programs of curricula around the issues of race relations and the causes and effects of racial disparity.

More resources provided for indigent defense will ensure better, more equal, representation. Changes in the distribution of resources are often legislatively driven and depend on local circumstances which vary from state to state. Two areas where inequitable resources for defense causes can lead to disparate treatment are: the timing of the assignment of counsel and the inability for the defense to advocate for and be thoroughly familiar with, alternative and creative dispositions at sentencing.

The limitations on funding for public defenders or court appointed attorneys often cause many jurisdictions to delay the appointment of counsel until after the initial arraignment appearance. This creates a problem for effective representation since many critical decisions are made at that stage of the adjudication process including the charge, the plea offer, the plea itself, and the bail/ release decision, which may, in turn, profoundly influence the outcomes at each of the subsequent stages of the process.

Assuring timely and effective representation immediately after arrest is certainly in the interests of poor, minority defendants whose over-representation in the system may be the most obvious example of disparate treatment. This is an issue which clearly illustrates the need for a close alliance between prosecutors and defense counsel as the timing and conditions of bail and the "rules of engagement" regarding plea negotiations are two of the most critical decision points in the system where disparity can be reduced.

In recent years, court systems across the country have witnessed the emergence of various types of "therapeutic" courts, such as drug courts, domestic violence courts and community courts. The common thread is that these courts seek to fashion dispositions and sanctions that offer assistance to the parties in addressing some of the problems that underlie the alleged offending. However, the publicly supported defender offices that staff these and other criminal courts are often severely lacking in resources to develop and advocate for dispositions and sentences that are likely to protect the public and address the needs of the defendant. This dearth of defense resources limits the extent to which these alternative approaches can be used for the vast majority of criminal defendants who are poor, and a substantial proportion of whom are members of various racial and ethnic minorities.

One of the primary ways that defense counsel can actively pursue the reduction of racial disparity is through the local Bar and Criminal Defense Attorney Associations. These associations can be organized to become active on the issue in several ways which would become the subject of ongoing training and education. The goal of this training is to educate, analyze and improve the way defense attorneys understand and deal with the problems of racial disparity. Other issues which the Bar and Criminal Defense Attorney Associations could address are:

— The development and implementation of standards and guidelines for bail, pretrial release, prosecutorial diversion, charge and plea bargaining.

— The development and funding of specific efforts to reduce minority representation at all stages of the justice process.

— The availability of other resource needs such as community-based alternative sanctions and sentencing advocacy opportunities.

The Judiciary

— Judges can provide important leadership in encouraging a research process similar to that described earlier in this manual to determine if minority defendants are treated disparately at:

 — arrest

 — the bail/release decision

 — in the assignment of defense attorneys

 — in diversion decisions, in the plea negotiation process

 — in the management of the court docket

 — at sentencing.

It is appropriate and desirable for judges to take a lead in discussions with representatives of the other system components, and representatives of minority communities, to identify factors that may contribute to disparity, and to develop and implement measures to correct disparity.

Expand the Range of Available Bail and Sentencing Options

— Institute training for judges on bail and sentencing decisions that examine not only the legal framework for judicial discretion but also provide specific education on improved pre-sentence investigation approaches by the defense, probation or some other agency, available alternatives to incarceration and eligibility requirements, enrollment procedures, etc.

— Work with other criminal justice officials and representatives of minority communities in designing and implementing useful and effective alternative pretrial release and post-adjudication sanction programs, in order to have a fuller array of options available to the bench.

— Work with local criminal justice and elected officials to consider how to address disparities in pretrial release and sentencing whereby defendants with access to resources (e.g., ability to pay for electronic monitoring or to privately enroll in a drug treatment program) are more likely to secure less punitive outcomes than those with lesser means.

— Maintain familiarity with scholarly and research literature documenting the processes that contribute to disparities, and use these findings appropriately in rulings on pretrial motions.

— Require pre-sentence say from probation officers that connect defendants with services and treatments necessary to avoid continued legal involvement; request detailed sentencing plans and proposals for alternatives to incarceration from defense counsel in serious cases.

— At sentencing, examine the role that racially-biased decisionmaking at prior stages of the criminal justice system may have played in relationship to arrest, charging, and plea decisions.

Take any such unwarranted disparities into account in reaching a sentencing decision.

— Articulate the court's expectations for ineffective assistance of counsel for all defendants and communicate these to practicing defense attorneys.

Leadership Development

— Judges can influence decisions to advance persons of color and leaders on racial disparity issues throughout court administrative structure.

— Encourage the local bench to participate in national judicial initiatives which are addressing racial disparities. For example, the National Judicial Conference is developing a Judges' Bench Book which will include information on the issue of racial disparity.

Public Education

— Judicial officials can encourage the media - especially the print media - to examine issues of racial disparity and the potential and planning for reforms.

— Provide public forums, such as "demonstration courts," to show the public how the court system works and to communicate "zero tolerance" stance against racial disparity.

— Examine role of continuing education for the judiciary and determine opportunities for racial, class and gender sensitivity training. For example, a session might focus on the economic realities of offenders who are facing bail requirements and how they impact persons of color.

— Courts should speak out to the public about the outcomes and impact of mandatory sentencing laws, and the advantages of restoring judicial discretion to make effective use of an expanded array of sentencing alternatives, sentencing statutes and sentencing guidelines. ! Welcome "court watchers" to examine, monitor and judicial behavior in terms of fair treatment to persons of color and others.

Judges have the opportunity to assess the cumulative impact of decisionmaking by criminal justice practitioners on how defendants are charged and what types of sentences are recommended. For example, federal judges can use a downward departure in a federal sentencing guidelines case for an African American man convicted of gun possession after observing that the offender's prior convictions include a number of minor traffic offenses that reflect the fact that as a black man he is more likely to be stopped by the police, therefore increasing his criminal history score more so than would be the case for a similarly situated white offender.

The development and implementation of a full range of sentencing options for use as alternatives to incarceration by the judiciary is fundamental to reducing racial disparity. The ability for the judiciary to use these alternatives at sentencing is equally critical. Trial court judges have considerable authority over actions and the expressed attitudes of the attorneys who appear before them. A trial court is not expected to tolerate dereliction of duty or disrespect, or disruption of court processes by any attorney. The trial court has the responsibility to maintain the dignity and propriety of all proceedings. A trial judge should correct misbehavior or any disruption by an attorney, disciplining the attorney if necessary.

The court's authority certainly extends to defense attorneys who use racist or other derogatory language or display such tendencies during their examination of a witness or argument. When attorneys fail to conform their behavior to the reasonable expectations of the court, they may be held in contempt and otherwise sanctioned. This authority extends to attorneys who take advantage or exploit a defendant's race to advantage before a jury.

Judges have a particular obligation to be attentive to counsel's conduct during jury selection. The court should permit voir dire to be thorough enough to disclose grounds for challenges for cause and to facilitate the intelligent exercise of each side's peremptory challenges. But the "intelligent exercise of peremptory challenges" does not extend to the use of peremptory challenges to eliminate racial diversity in a jury panel. With or without objection by either party, a court should not permit use of peremptory challenges to remove a prospective juror for reasons which are constitutionally suspect.

The judiciary has other means of strengthening its own constitutional commitment to reducing racial disparity. In most states, the highest court describes rules to help guide and control judicial conduct in the lower courts. Utilizing studies or research data demonstrating racial disparity at one or more stages of the criminal court process, judicial agencies (often the state supreme court) should adopt rules which will achieve judicial and law enforcement objectives in criminal procedures while reducing disparity in application and outcomes.

Judicial education is one of the most critical elements in the fight against racial disparity. Vigorous training programs should be established by organizations responsible for judicial training. These should focus on the varieties of sentencing theory, the range of sentencing options which various theories call for, the nature of the sentencing options actually available in that jurisdiction, and how they can be utilized by the judge in his or her courtroom.

It is important to understand that relationships between judges and defendants/offenders can make a difference. Offenders can be affected by the realization that judges are trying to help them and are concerned about their problems. The personal consideration that is frequently extended to the privileged defendant is a model for individualized treatment that should be offered to all defendants. Judges can help by managing dockets and arranging schedules to address public defender workloads by, for example, arranging for them to have a day free of court appearances for client contact. Judges can similarly provide time for the defense and presentation to conference cases in a less frantic manner than often occurs during normal court hours. These strategies could be included in new judge training on docket management.

Judges can stimulate public discussions among court officials and the public. For example, following on a report from Northeastern University that minority suspects charged with drug offenses were more likely to be prosecuted on distribution charges than white suspects in similar circumstances, a judge convened a working group of police, prosecutors, and minority community leaders to determine whether the race of a defendant played a role in how drug cases are charged. Judges can initiate studies of their jurisdiction's pretrial release and sentencing practices and respond with judicial education programs that include courses designed to eliminate bias in pretrial release and sentencing. These programs can examine how unconscious biases may affect judges' ability to deal equitably with persons unlike the judge - whether different by race, sex, class, sexual orientation, or political orientation.

PROBATION

— Probation officials, with the assistance of other criminal justice personnel and representatives of minority communities, should carefully review their policies, practices, guidelines, and supervisory systems to identify those factors that dictate the kinds of information they collect on defendants, and the ways in which that information is interpreted in:

— preparing presentence reports

— making sentencing recommendations

— seeking community-based services for potential and current probationers

— monitoring and interpreting the behavior of persons under supervision

— applying graduated sanctions to non-compliant probationers

— initiating probation violation proceedings.

Those influencing factors that may impact negatively on minority group members should be identified and modified to reduce their disparate effects.

— Analyze the presentation of pre-sentence reports on an ongoing basis to determine whether the style and language used in them differs by race or ethnicity of the offender. If so, initiate appropriate training measures to eliminate any unintended bias in such presentations.

Reorient Probation Services to a Community-Based Model

— There is a need to be aware of any social and cultural distance between probation personnel and the people whom they investigate and supervise. Toward that end, probation departments should decentralize their operations into the communities where their caseloads are concentrated.

— Decentralized personnel should focus on developing effective working relationships with local faith-based organizations, civic organizations, and social service agencies to assist in developing more individualized presentence reports, in providing services to probationers, in connecting these local agencies to effective working relationships with the courts, and in developing a range of graduated sanctions for non-compliant probationers, to reduce revocations where appropriate.

— Decentralized personnel should work with police, other criminal justice agencies, and neighborhood organizations, to solve some of the community problems that produce high rates of crime and arrests. The Boston juvenile gang model, in which probation officers work with police officers to meet with high-risk youth probationers and their families at home, seems particularly promising.

— Probation officers need to work outside the office and outside office hours to be more accessible to their clients and able to intervene early to problem solve.

Develop a Range of Sanctions for Non-Compliance Relapse

— A range of effective graduated sanctions for non-compliance, and relapse responses to drug abusing probationers, is especially important to reduce the number of probation violators who are being incarcerated, and to provide realistic assistance along a path to a more law-abiding life.

— Assess whether minorities may require additional services to maintain compliance, including employment, substance abuse, and others, and focus the resources of probation to respond accordingly.

— Examine and improve as needed policies and processes for handling probation violations so that they are based on neutral and objective assessments of risk and driven by structured guidelines which standardize as much as possible the criteria for and response to violations and which are continually monitored.

— Examine "relapse prevention model" for offender supervision and institute approaches (policies, procedures, programs, demonstration models) to weave this model into the current structure of probation supervision and enforcement.

Develop and Utilize Race Neutral Risk Management Assessments

— Institute well-researched, structured, neutral and objective assessments for risk management to determine levels of supervision which are continually monitored, and provide appropriate training for their use.

— Evaluate the impact of these tools on a regular basis to determine whether there are any unintended racial disparities.

Leadership Development

— Develop aggressive affirmative action policies for the recruitment, retaining and advancement of persons of color and those who portray leadership qualities around the issues of race, class and gender discrimination. Where civil service system requirements are paramount, it is especially important to recruit aggressively among communities of color for people to take civil service tests (e.g., through colleges and faith-based organizations), and to make sure that those tests are race neutral.

Advocate for Greater Public Support of Probation Services

— Examine relationship between lack of funding which drives high caseloads and the subsequent inability to provide quality services in a timely manner which ,in turn, may lead to disparate treatment based on race, class or gender. How can the quality of performance be maintained under difficult conditions? What is the impact of high caseloads on racial disparity?

— Probation agencies are notoriously under-funded and, within the criminal justice network, they are the most vulnerable to budget cuts. Yet their caseloads, in which minority offenders are over-represented, rise every year. To undertake the efforts recommended here, and to prevent the increasing confinement of minority offenders, it is crucial that probation agencies be provided with more adequate levels of funding.

The goals and objectives of probation agencies are in a period of transition today regarding the appropriate balance between enforcement/supervision and treatment. Neither role can be done well without access to the full range of human services available in the community. In recent years, more policymakers have argued that probation officers should be brokers of services as they are not equipped to provide treatment themselves. One unintended consequence of this is that probation agents are becoming more like law enforcement, rather than case managers - despite the fact that they have higher caseloads in need of services. At the same time, human service agencies are relying more on the criminal justice system to handle difficult cases rather than cooperating to provide services while probation provides supervision.

This lack of resources and the need for more sophisticated policies to guide their use, can lead to disparate treatment of minorities who are under probation supervision. In order to address the issue, policymakers must provide guidance on the criteria which will be used to recommend services - such as more structured drug treatment as a response to relapse rather than revocation - and a much broader commitment to accessing existing and new services in the areas of treatment, vocational training, education and employment.

Discretion must be exercised by supervising agents who, in turn, need effective standards for assessment and classification decisions, structuring the size and char cteristics of caseloads, conducting supervision and monitoring, and making decisions regarding which offender clients receive specific services. In the absence of effective standards and supervisory accountability systems, these decisions are vulnerable to excessive subjectivity and inadvertent bias. For example, the frequency of drug testing and the range of responses allowed are often subjective and they need to be controlled by standards for application and response which are race neutral.

Goals and objectives regarding drug use that are based on a relapse prevention model, rather than detection, can aid in moving toward more successful community-based outcomes for offenders. This requires broad-based education of not only probation agents but judges and prosecutors as well. The purpose of the presentence investigation needs to be refocused. An individualized model assessing both the circumstances contributing to the offense and exploring community-based sentencing options will produce different outcomes than more limited reports that primarily focus only on the offense itself. Judges and probation offices can work cooperatively so that judges articulate what they need from presentence investigations to help them with disposition, focusing on specific information such as drug use, mental health, and risk assessment, and the availability of community-based treatment and service programs. If the sentencing judge dismisses the probation officer's recommendation, s/he should do so with consideration for the probation officer's position, validating the officer so s/he does not feel undermined or have the relationship with the client damaged.

Probation agencies must determine if their offices will operate on an enforcement model or a broker of services/ case management model and hire accordingly. The recruitment process for probation officers is as important as their training and education at each stage. A fundamental step in avoiding disparity is recruiting probation officers who believe in due process.

Crucial to the role of probation agencies in developing approaches to reduce racial disparity is to gain the support and involvement of other agencies, organizations and interest groups. In essence, to engage the community in its work to provide fair and racially sensitive services to offenders under their supervision. The American Probation and Parole Association has recently adopted a national policy for its members that will require critical changes to the way that probation agencies do business. This policy, called "Broken Windows Probation," calls for the practice of inclusivity - both formally and informally - when probation administrators develop policies, initiate programs, develop supervision strategies and deliver services. This policy should do much to help reduce racial disparity because the organizations which represent public opinion on the need to reduce disparity will be involved in the process. The recommendations of the APPA include the following suggestions for local probation offices, which are further encouraged to reduce racial disparity:

— Create a system that has meaningful participation for victims and the community;

— Develop partnerships with neighborhood groups, schools, businesses, and faith communities to bring offenders into an environment that has pro-social supports and structure;

— Establish cooperative partnerships among probation, law enforcement, and other criminal justice agencies that focus on public safety and the related issue of racial disparity;

— Partner with human service, treatment, and non-profit agencies to provide enhanced services to assess, diagnose, treat, and supervise offenders; and,

— Create a comprehensive education campaign to make citizens aware of the crime problem, and the related issue of racial disparity, the steps being taken to address it, and the communication that their involvement is needed and desired.

Jails and Prisons

— While fair treatment is an important concern for everyone, its importance is intensified for those held in total institutions like jails and prisons. Given the predominantly minority composition of the inmate population, and the predominantly white composition of the custodial staff and managers, sensitivity to perceived racial bias is especially problematic in these institutions. Therefore, it is important that both the staff and the inmates in each institution are provided with assurance that the issue of racial disparity in treatment is an important concern of the administration.

Toward that end, the administration in each institution should form a working party consisting of a representative from each department in the institution and inmate representatives to review all policies and practices to assure that everything necessary is being done to guard against racially disparate treatment of inmates. To the extent that racially disparate outcomes are identified, the administration should develop policies or practices that can achieve the institution's objectives while reducing unwarranted disparities. The review should focus on at least the following key decisions affecting inmate life:

— Inmate risk assessments and classification;

— Assessments of inmates' alcohol and drug dependency;

— Assessments of inmates' mental health needs;

— Inmate access to libraries, gyms, and other facilities in the institution;

— Inmate access to treatment for alcohol and chemical dependency;

— Inmate access to physical and mental health services;

— Inmate access to religious and counseling services;

— Inmate access to educational and skill development services;

— Inmate access to work and educational release programs;

— Consideration of dietary and religious preferences in menu preparation;

— Development of rules for inmate behavior;

— Application of the disciplinary system to inmates;

— Inmate access to community services upon release.

Monitor Racial Tensions in Institutions

— Establish a plan for the routine monitoring of racial tensions between staff and inmates, and among various groups of inmates, and for regular presentation of programs designed to reduce those tensions.

— Establish a plan for the routine monitoring of gang formation and inter-group hostilities among the inmates, and for regular interventions to discourage gang formation and diffuse inter-group hostilities.

Affirmative Action in Recruiting and Leadership

— Ensure there are sufficient numbers of staff of same race as prisoners to promote understanding of the needs and points of view of different racial groups and to give system credibility and legitimacy.

— Develop aggressive affirmative action policies for the recruitment, retaining and advancement of persons of color and those who portray leadership qualities around the issues of race, class and gender discrimination.

Utilize Community Resources to Augment Services

— Establish mechanisms that enable the social service staff to work effectively with faith-based organizations and service organizations in communities from which significant segments of the inmate population come to facilitate communication, family visiting, and referral to community services upon release.

— Develop with parole authorities the nine essential components for successful offender reintegration.

Similar to probation, discretion on the part of supervising personnel (guards, case managers) can lead to disparate treatment. Without the development and regular review of standards for assessment, case levels, supervision and monitoring, decisions regarding which offender clients receive specific services are subjective and open for disparity. Jail and prison administrators are encouraged to examine the use of discretion in areas of job and housing assignments, inmate disciplinary action, strip and cell searches, and drug testing, and to institute race sensitive neutral, objective, structured and validated guidelines for the exercise of discretion. Suggestions include:

— Establish policies, procedures and reporting requirements

— Identify criteria for use of discretion, e.g. drug testing of specific prisoner

— Provide for supervisor review of reports

— Provide independent appeal or grievance procedure

— Identify both legal requirements and progressive practices

— Use resources provided by professional associations such as standards, accreditation and best practices

— Develop a credible grievance process with links to central office so that complaints can be monitored and are not lost.

— Insure that Internal Affairs investigators are sensitive to racial dynamics within facility and are themselves a diverse group to give credibility to investigations.

— Install video cameras in less public locations where incidents are likely to occur.

— Insist on zero tolerance for acts of overt discrimination and intolerance. Racial tension (especially between staff and prisoners) creates a security risk. Threats to order and stability through staff behavior cannot be tolerated.

— Provide appropriate, high-quality, well-structured training to sensitize staff to racial issues.

— Encourage chief executive/key decision maker to include questions on racial disparity and strategies to address it when considering appointment of senior staff.

Effective Management Information Systems are essential to monitor changes in overall agency behavior. Tracking and reporting mechanisms for decision points are essential. Auditing for adherence to policies should include measurement of racial disparities. Corrections policies should reduce uses of discretion which can lead to discriminatory behavior. For example, classification criteria and decisions which may not be race neutral need to be examined to determine their effect on disparity. This is particularly important because of the connection between institutional conduct and release decisions.

While not in itself discriminatory, the lack of in-prison programming which can reduce the likelihood of relapse upon release is a serious deficiency, particularly in light of the fact that some offenders may prefer to max out their time to avoid post-release supervision - especially of their drug use. Jail and prison administrators are thus encouraged to become familiar with the "What Works?" literature, which has identified "guiding principles for effective correctional intervention". These principles, if enacted as overarching policy goals and the subject of intensified training can do much to reduce the negative effects of incarceration and disparity which may be present in the criminal processing of offenders.

Parole

— Parole administrators should establish a working group of parole commissioners, parole officers, supervisors and managers, and parolee representatives to review policies and practices that influence:

— decisions regarding parole release

— the development and imposition of the parole release plan and conditions

— the monitoring of parolee compliance

— the decision to violate the parolee for non-compliance.

— The review should focus on identifying ways in which the factors influencing these decisions may produce racially disparate effects, and on the development of appropriate corrective measures when this is the case.

— Parole authorities should carefully review revocation practices and, with the aid of service organizations in the community, construct a system of graduated sanctions for responding to noncompliance.

— Parole authorities should establish protocols to monitor and analyze parole violations processing, cross-referenced by race to determine if patterns of discrimination are apparent.

— Paroling authorities should assess whether minorities may require additional services to maintain compliance, including employment, substance abuse, and others, and locate the resources to respond accordingly.

Establish Relationships with Community-Based Organizations

— Parole administrators should establish effective working relationships with faith-based organizations and public and private service organizations in communities in which significant numbers of parolees reside. These organizations may then become actively involved in developing a release plan for persons about to be paroled, and in providing needed services to the parolee to assist in his or her re-integration in the community.

— Parole offices should be decentralized to these communities to assist parole officers to learn about and become known in the community. This will facilitate their efforts to involve the community in assisting the parolee to make a positive adjustment.

Develop Relationships with other Criminal Justice Agencies

— Encourage paroling authorities to interact on a regular basis with prosecutors and judges on issues of race and racial disparity. Cross-system training opportunities should be identified and pursued.

Develop Race-Neutral Risk Management Assessments

— Institute well-researched, structured, neutral and objective assessments for risk management to determine levels of supervision which are continually monitored.

Assure Diversity of Leadership and Orientation

— Appoint Parole Boards that are racially and culturally diverse.

— Provide racial and cultural sensitivity training for Parole Board members, as well as parole officers and supervisors, and encourage broad-based interaction with the professional community and general public on racial and ethnic issues.

Paroling agencies are under increased pressures to balance the political and public safety concerns of inmate release with the realities of prison crowding. But within this context, attention must be paid to the allocation of resources to helping people when they come out of prison and back into the community. Arrangements for post prison transition must deal realistically with the poor coping skills that contribute to offenders' return to prison. Support systems need to be put in place involving business and the private sector.

Cross-system Integration

The primary obstacle to successful post-release transition of alcohol and drug addicted prison inmates is a lack of system integration between the releasing institution and the community (housing, employment, health care, treatment). In order to improve cross-system integration:

— The offenders' problems and needs should be seen as the responsibility of both systems with offender success benefiting both systems.

— Systems-wide planning should take place at both the state and local level.

— Joint case planning - driven by screening and assessments of offender treatment and ancillary needs- must be an integral component of the projects.

— There must be established protocols for sharing case information.

— A "boundary spanner" or "case manager" must be in place to negotiate specific offender case management variables regardless of the setting (i.e. prison or the community). The boundary spanner should be a community-based position with access to the in-prison components of the project.

— On-going case training is needed in both systems.

— Creative contracts and letters of agreement must delineate the responsibilities of both parties.

Essential Components for Successful Offender Re-integration

The linkages between the institution and the community must be clear, strong and delineated in writing before the program is implemented. Agreements between institution and community-based service providers, regardless of who they work for, should address several issues:

— Recognition by service providers that system linkages and case management are essential.

— A shared statement of common goals and objectives.

— Multi disciplinary teams (such as welfare, supervision, child protective custody, drug/alcohol/mental health treatment) working from the same case management plan regardless of the setting (i.e. prison, community, court, parole, etc.).

— Clear documented protocols for institutions and community service providers that specify how continuity of services will take place

— Agreements for assessments, case management planning, and case management services.

— The provision of a full range of services which are matched to individual need and are driven by standardized assessments provided by qualified and trained staff.

— A unified approach to relapse prevention and response to predictable relapse.

— Case managers that span the boundaries of all systems (i.e. institutional and community).

— Ability to move from less to more intensive sanctions/services pursuant to offender behavior.

Adult offender systems that include safe "middle ground" housing can provide control without secure confinement prior to full release to the community. These supportive and controlled environments offer an opportunity to deal with the issues often associated with return to prison-usually drug relapse and lack of quality employment-and would have an impact on racial disparity issues if for no other reason than the overrepresentation of minorities in the nation's jails and prisons.

Similar to issues in probation and institutions, discretion on the part of parole agents can lead to disparate treatment: without standards for assessment, case levels, supervision and monitoring, the decisions regarding which offender clients receive specific services is subjective.

Many officials receive inadequate education about the use of random drug testing as an appropriate trigger for reincarceration. This may be particularly important in jurisdictions which are experiencing prison crowding. When the systems are crowded there may be an informal understanding not to be so quick to revoke parole - discretion at this stage may also reflect biases. Increasing the use of revocation without standardized graduated sanctions can lead to both greater use of incarceration and disparities.

Systemwide and Legislative Options

While leaders at each level of the criminal justice system have a responsibility to address and reduce unwarranted racial disparity, a systemic and comprehensive approach by all parts of the system is critical if disparities are to be addressed effectively. There are two primary reasons for this:

Most decision points in the criminal justice system reflect input and actions from various actors in the system and so require a coordinated response. For example, sentencing decisions reflect input and/or advocacy from a probation presentence report, prosecutor, defense, and ultimately the judiciary.

Because outcomes are dependent on various actors, progress in one component of the system can be offset by decisions made in another area. Law enforcement efforts designed to reduce the use of "racial profiling," for example, may be offset by a mayoral proclamation to "get tough on drugs" which results in increasing arrests in minority communities.

Legislative actions will also have a major effect on systemwide options. This may be a negative if new laws have a discriminatory impact but legislative support of systemwide reforms, as in the examples below from Connecticut and North Carolina, will greatly enhance their likelihood of success. Systemwide efforts to address racial disparities can include the following set of activities:

Data Collection and Analysis

— Use existing planning forums, such as community corrections boards or criminal justice coordinating councils, to examine the issue and provide planning opportunities to address it.

— Assess the degree to which disparity is evident at each stage of the administration of justice and as an end result.

— Examine the utility of local Management Information Systems to determine the scope of the issue and ability to monitor changes to the system after reforms are initiated.

— Explore how technology affects disparity; for example, does the use of video arraignment help or hinder persons of color or low economic status?

Collaborative Actions

— Develop a framework for assessing which actors have input into each decision-making point of the system.

— Provide oversight and monitoring at each decision point of the system to examine, reduce, and track disparity.

— Establish a timetable, objectives, and strategy for reducing disparities at each stage of the system.

— Collaborate with national and state organizations and associations to develop model codes, guidelines, and policies to reduce disparities.

— Call for strong leadership to: a) Improve the quality of justice; b) Improve race relations and the social compact; and c) Reduce crime and improve the community's quality of life.

— Implement a "zero tolerance" agreement among key system actors that decision-making will be conducted in a race neutral fashion and disparity will be reduced wherever possible.

— Establish a systemwide agreement that, while discretion is critical to the administration of justice, its objective and effective use is essential for fairness. Standards, guidelines, and policies for the use of discretion can be applied at each point along the continuum, along with systems for monitoring.

9

Surveillance and Detection

The technical advances in the detection and processing of offenders, which have underpinned the expansion of the infringement notice system, also have significant civil liberties implications. These relate to the intrusiveness and propriety of the surveillance techniques used to detect and record breaches of the law; the question of who should be granted access to those techniques; whether the data thus gathered should be amalgamated with other material so as to be available in larger, more comprehensive, databases used for other purposes; and whether these advances in automating criminal justice are producing untoward changes in policing methods and in the courts.

The advances in technology have the capacity, not yet fully realised, to be used proactively in many areas of law enforcement. They can keep large sectors of the population under surveillance as they engage in activities which may have an impact on road safety, the well-being of the environment, public order, and safety, and financial and commercial transactions. Cameras are no longer confined to catching motorists. They are being focussed on potential offenders in the stands and galleries of sporting arenas,they are used in public and private areas to monitor perimeter security, maintain stock control, and preserve public safety, and they can be found in malls, railway stations, banks, and other areas in which remote and/or continuous sensing for preventive purposes is thought to be needed. Police already regard the film record of red light cameras as open to scrutiny in the investigation of more serious offences, such as causing death by culpable driving or hit-run accidents. It is not difficult to conceive how the movement of particular vehicles or persons as registered by cameras designed to pick up motoring offences might also be of interest to other investigatory agencies, such as the National Crime Authority, with whom local police routinely exchange information.

As the merit of particular technical innovations becomes apparent and the cost of accessing the technology falls, reliance on the devices tends to increase.Though many of the devices started off as aids to the replacement of subjective measures of liability with objective ones, the crime prevention objective has encouraged their use as mass screening devices for groups thought to be at risk of offending. This shift in usage is well illustrated by the impact of the breathalyser in detecting drink impaired drivers.

As an indicator of intoxication, the readings of these machines were vastly more convenient than those which depended on having to obtain blood or urine samples for laboratory analysis. They also provided results almost instantaneously. They were less vulnerable to attack than the earlier purely subjective tests of intoxication. As confidence in the technology increased, the subjective measures of impairment and the concept of drunkenness itself were abandoned in favour of an assumption of impairment once a legislatively specified minimum concentration of alcohol in the blood had been reached.

Nowadays, the actus reus of drink-driving offences is expressed in terms of driving with a minimum concentration of alcohol in the blood as measured by a specified type of breathalyser machine. While the new technology made it much easier to establish liability in particular cases, this was not enough to satisfy the broader preventive goals of policing. Soon afterwards, simpler and more portable breath analysis machines became available. Though these were less accurate than the more sophisticated breathalyser, they were employed as the screening device for the random 'preliminary breath test' which, in Victoria, is used in conjunction with 'booze buses' to quickly assess the state of alcohol impairment of groups of drivers randomly pulled out of the main stream of passing traffic.

A diagnostic instrument has been converted into a screening device and deployed in relation to a much larger target population. Moreover, this screening process has spawned subsidiary offences pertaining to refusal to submit to these random tests. Because the larger number of tests administered in screening for offenders produced a greater number of cases requiring adjudication, the majority of offences came to be defined as infringements so they could be dealt with by way of on-the-spot tickets, rather than a summons to court.

This scenario is typical of the changing uses to which the new technology is put. Technical innovations offer simplicity and efficiency in gathering evidence of wrongdoing. But there are countervailing considerations. First, while some of the technology can gather evidence of offending by unobtrusive means, others involve the alleged offender or the segment of the population being screened, in submitting to some degree of inconvenience and self-incrimination.

Second, even when the surveillance and detection techniques are more covert, less visible and, as with photographic detection devices, least intrusive, the invasion of a citizen's privacy and autonomy represented by these techniques may be regarded as all the more insidious because that intrusion has come in a covert, largely invisible, electronic form. The citizen has little notice of being under surveillance, and usually receives no immediate indication that he or she has been detected. Third, the new technology could, in theory, be used to detect and convict every person who breached a particular rule in an area of close surveillance.Such vigorous enforcement would be regarded as oppressive and involving excessive labelling of large numbers of citizens as offenders.

Total compliance with prohibitions on lesser offences is never expected and can be pursued at too great a price in terms of public support for the law and goodwill towards the enforcement officials. Respect for rights of privacy and self-determination is based, in part, on the practical reality that not all the law is enforced all the time.This assumption of the reasonable enforcement of the law is undermined when rigorous enforcement of the law is made easier. Not only does the new technology lower costs and increase efficiency, but the threshold of enforcement intervention can be reduced. In the past, only the more extreme speedsters were pursued by police. Now speed cameras sweep up droves of drivers travelling only marginally above the speed limit. Fourth, the legislation which supports the technology makes the evidence gathered almost legally unassailable.

Breach of the law becomes defined in terms of the data gathered by the instrument itself, rather than the actual conduct being observed. The evidence gathered becomes impervious to attack because it is supported by legal presumptions that the information produced by the instrument proves what it claims to represent. It forecloses the need for further investigation or analysis and stymies most defences. In the case of red-light cameras, photographic evidence of guilt is usually so clear that almost no legal challenge is possible and the burden of a fact-determining trial is treated as superfluous. The shift from judicial to administrative findings of guilt thus gains momentum. Fifth, the pressure placed on alleged offenders to admit guilt provides police and other enforcement authorities with an incentive to charge offences that would not have been justified if a full judicial hearing were required, and proof had to be established by conventional means.

Cases in which a warning might have been administered, or which would have proved difficult or expensive to have established forensically, can now be pursued easily and conveniently under the infringement notice system. Sixth, as has already been demonstrated, in relation to the difficulties with the Sheriff's Office, the technology may detect more offenders than the compliance system can cope with, thus leading to delays, inefficiencies, ill-will, and loss of revenue that may exceed the fiscal or other benefits allegedly attained by introducing the technology in the first place.

Technological capacities

Detection: The sanctions which accompany an infringement notice will produce no deterrent effect unless potential offenders believe that there is a significant risk of being detected. Citizens fully understand that a large number of infringements go undetected. Drivers who speed, people who dump litter, owners of unrestrained dogs, by-law violators, and others who commit summary offences all recognise that they have a better than even chance of breaking the law with impunity. They know that the law is a 'punitive lottery'and gamble upon it regularly. To overcome this perception that there is a good chance of avoiding liability requires a marked improvement in the actual rate of detection, or in what is perceived as the probability of detection.

The main technological developments affecting the infringement notice system have their impact at this detection stage, primarily in relation to motoring offences. Though the technical advances on this front have been considerable, all the possibilities have not yet been realised. For instance, the original 1988 evaluations of the utility of speed cameras for Victoria suggested that, in the future, the cameras might be deployed in permanent in-ground unmanned detectors, in a fashion similar to the unmanned red light cameras, in order to screen all passing traffic.

The cameras would no longer need to be manned by individual police operators, and, if purchased and installed in bulk, could provide a vastly expanded area of continuous surveillance. This idea was regarded as worthy of support by the Victorian Parliament's Social Development Committee in its inquiry into speed limits in Victoria.Speed is not the only characteristic of a vehicle that can be evaluated by unmanned sensors.

Other characteristics of the vehicle, such as its emissions and mass, can also be monitored. The former are relevant to environment protection and anti-pollution legislation and the latter to offences involving overloading and safety. Overloading offences are particularly significant to commercial transport vehicles which ply the highways. Devices already exist for measuring a moving vehicle's height, length and mass.

The New South Wales government, through its Roads and Traffic Authority, has introduced an Australian designed satellite surveillance scheme originally called 'Scamcam', but later renamed 'Safe- T-Cam', which uses special infra-red roadside cameras to read the registration plates of passing trucks.The data is checked immediately by computers linked to the sensor via satellite to identify whether there are any outstanding warrants against the vehicle's owner, or whether the vehicle is of interest to the police for any other reason.At the same time, the camera can be used with other devices, to check the speed and weight of the passing vehicle. The information can be processed quickly and the sensors are located on the highway between turn-offs so as to allow the vehicle to be apprehended further down the road once the analysis of the information indicates the vehicle is worthy of attention.

The external detection devices can be supplemented by internal ones which allow a vehicle to 'incriminate' itself. Of special interest are the vehicle monitoring devices which are the equivalent of the 'black box' installed in modern commercial aircraft. These maintain a continuous record of the main features of the operation of the vehicle or aircraft. In the case of motor vehicles, the monitoring devices record starting and stopping times, acceleration and braking, and speed. If connected to load-sensing devices built into the vehicle itself, especially in commercial vehicles, the weight of the load being carried at any particular time can also be registered.

Although originally designed to assist owners of commercial heavy vehicles to monitor the behaviour of their drivers, it is now clear that the quality of information recorded in the monitoring devices and the security of the devices themselves, lend themselves to enforcement purposes.

The ability of authorised persons to access the record, means that enforcement agencies interested in the behaviour of a vehicle on the road can identify the salient features, after the event, without having to engage in on-road detection either through external monitoring devices, or highway patrols. The installation of sealed vehicle monitoring devices of this type could be made compulsory and the data routinely and electronically downloaded for computerised analysis to detect infringements. Thus, if the instrument recorded the vehicle travelling above the speed limit at any point in the journey, an infringement notice could be issued. Both the analysis of the behaviour of the vehicle and the issue of the infringement notice could be entirely computerised. The significance of this goes beyond mere reduction of enforcement costs.

Penalties do not need to be severe simply in order to offset the uncertainty of detection. They could therefore be set at the minimum level needed to offset the economic incentive for non-compliance, or at a level that recoups the full cost of the unlawful conduct. In the latter case the penalty assumes the character of a tax.

Another idea is to build into each motor vehicle a unique electronic identifier, which could be used for the automatic electronic interrogation of vehicles. This could be paired with the similar idea of requiring all drivers to carry a 'Smartcard' identification device. Both respond electronically to interrogation by static detection devices which could be also linked to speed cameras and the like. It would thus be possible to identify both the vehicle and the driver at the time of offending.

Electronic driver identification allows a more precise allocation of responsibility for non-complying conduct and would reduce the need to rely upon owner-onus provisions with all the difficulties which these produce, particularly in relation to vehicles owned by corporations.

It is also conceivable that the built-in vehicle identification devices would be capable of being switched on by enforcement officials in the event of the vehicle being reported stolen as an aid to its location. They might also be designed to incapacitate a vehicle. Already proposals are in place for 'drunk locks' on car ignitions for convicted drink-driver offenders.An electro-chemical sensor would bar ignition until the driver blows a breath registering below 0.5 blood alcohol content. This interlock has been under consideration in Victoria since the mid-1980s. The installation of interlocks, vehicle identification devices and the carrying of drivers' licences with built-in 'Smartcard' electronics could readily be made compulsory by law.

Three elements underlie all of the technological innovations in the automatic detection of offences. First, a unit to detect and measure the particular feature of interest, e.g. speed, weight, photo-chemical emissions etc; secondly, a device for recording the identity of the offender picked up by the detector unit; and thirdly, a triggering device set so as to activate the recording only when the detector exceeds a pre-determined threshold.

Each of these three elements is capable of improvement in the light of technological advances. Furthermore, advances in the way in which the elements can be combined with each other and with the arrangements of issuing infringement notices to the person regarded in law as responsible for the offence, allow for that process to take place in a faster, more integrated and more highly automated fashion.

For instance, the newest forms of speed cameras, about to be introduced in Australia, use digital computer images instead of film to record the offending vehicle. In fact, they take two images simultaneously, one a regular wide-angle picture of the vehicle and, the second, a zoom shot of the number plate. Because the image is captured in a digital form on computer, it is capable of further enhancement in order to read the number plate. These cameras are not only cheaper to operate than film-based ones because the handling and processing of film is obviated, but also allow the digital image to be transferred electronically to a central office for processing and issuing of tickets. This can be done via a mobile phone, satellite dish, or direct landline.

It results in faster issue of infringement notices. Though encouraging the Victoria Police to continue with the testing and evaluation of new technology cameras, the Victorian Parliamentary Road Safety Committee, in its recent Inquiry Into the Demerit Points Scheme, expressed concern about the manner in which it is possible to manipulate the details of an image produced by modern computer imaging technology.

Also in the pipeline are the anti-pollution equivalents of speed cameras. These are devices for detecting unacceptable vehicle emissions and pollutants by passing an infra-red beam through exhaustfumes and using infra-red absorption technology to analyse the nature of those emissions and their levels.Also under consideration is the use of laser beams for more accurate detection of speed than is presently provided by the radar-based speed cameras. The laser beams would also be more efficient in reading number plates if the latter, by law, were required to incorporate a bar-code identifier.

Already railway rolling stock has bar-code tags attached which make the identification and location of individual wagons and carriages easier. Use of bar-code identifiers may not only obviate the need for intermediate photographic processing, but might even cut out the need for the on-line digital imaging systems which are just now beginning to be introduced.

Other existing road monitoring devices, such as vehicle sensing loops concealed under the tarmac of the road, may be improved and given new uses. Such sensing loops already are to be found in capital cities in Australia where they are used to monitor traffic flow for the purpose of adjusting the timing of traffic lights. Loops of this sort could also be used for the automatic electronic identification of vehicles and possibly drivers in the manner outlined above. However, one of the problems in cutting detectors into roadways, or installing them on roadsides, is that the road network is huge and growing continuously. Detectors cannot be located at all intersections, except at enormous cost. The further apart such devices are placed, the less is the deterrent effect. Some rules for strategic targeting of offenders are required.

Targeting: It is well within the capacity of the new technology to store, in a central registry, identifying data on offenders, vehicle owners, drivers' licence holders and to allow rapid access to that information by multiple authorised users. This offers the potential to monitor patterns of illegal behaviour with a view to targeting either particular geographical areas in which offences occur, or classes, types, or age groups of offender for selective enforcement.

If computerised information on infringement offences and other wrongdoing is matched against parallel information contained on computerised central registries in other jurisdictions within Australia, a national profile of offending can be drawn up. Likewise, if the data contained in relation to infringement offences is matched against other databases containing information on other forms of wrongdoing, such as those maintained by the Australian Securities Commission, or other national or local enforcement agencies, the analysis of the matched files may produce profiles relevant to more serious forms of misconduct.

Yet again, if the infringement notice data is linked with electoral, social security, or taxation records, it would speed up the location of fine defaulters, thus addressing a major problem within the infringement notice system. That matching is also, incidentally, likely to throw up evidence of other fiscal wrongdoing. The consolidation of databases would not only be useful for tracing defaulting drivers, it would also improve the tracing of vehicles owned by defaulters. The latter could then be seized and sold to meet outstanding fines. By storing information about breaches of the law for analysis by more sophisticated programs, systematic patterns of wrongdoing can be exposed, cross-references made, chronologies and inter-relationships exposed. This may be particularly valuable in the area of commercial transport, in that it may reveal a deliberate policy of breaching the law by commercial goods vehicles operators, which goes beyond that which can be remedied by the repeated imposition of infringement notices.

A sustained pattern of recidivism would indicate that prosecutorial discretion should be exercised in favour of court-based appearances rather than infringement notices. A larger range of more threatening sanctions could then be available to the enforcement agencies. Furthermore, concepts of incitement and complicity, not available at the infringement level, could allow the higher level officials who were responsible for the deliberate policy of breaking the law in the interests of commercial expediency to be joined for punishment.

Selective targeting of more serious or repeated offenders may become more important if the new technology for detecting the illegal behaviour generates unmanageable workloads in processing the extra offences detected. Although the technology can be readily adapted to have infringement notices, or summonses, rapidly issued and posted to the alleged offender, any significant degree of resistance to payment, or inaccuracy in the databases on which the identification of the offenders depends, will produce an unmanageably large backlog of enforcement problems.

Sanctions: In addition to improvements in detecting offenders, tracing of vehicles through computer-matching techniques and the possibility that financial penalties may be automatically added to vehicle registration fees, or directly debited from bank accounts, the new technology also offers the possibility of direct immobilisation of vehicles. The possibility exists of vehicles of the future incorporating tamper-proof electronic controls which allow their immobilisation through external controls operated by vehicle registration authorities or police. As has been discussed above,such devices have been mooted as a means of controlling drink-drivers.

One version, already discussed above, is the electrochemical sensor which requires the driver to pass a preliminary breath test before being able to engage the ignition of the motor vehicle. Another version depends upon the driver being too uncoordinated to be able to enter a set of numbers into a keypad in the dashboard within a short space of time. If the drink-driver fails to do so within the prescribed period, the electrical system of the vehicle will be isolated for some hours.

Both of these devices are open to being defeated by a person, other than the driver, passing the test for the intoxicated person. It is possible to envisage immobilising devices being fitted to vehicles and being triggered after a certain number of infringement notices have been recorded in relation to the use of the particular vehicle, or on non-payment of registration, or on the vehicle itself reaching a certain state of unroadworthiness, or being overloaded. If sanctions more severe than fines are to be applied for those who commit the more serious forms of infringement, techniques of electronic monitored home detention already exist and are in use in this country.

Entrapment

There is anxiety that the covert and surreptitious nature of the new detection devices allows them to be employed in settings that are inappropriate to achieving the desired deterrent effect and are being used in a manner which involves elements of instigation, incitement, or entrapment.

The point that speed cameras have often been placed in settings which do not appear to bear any relationship to the actual traffic danger represented by that location, has been forcibly made by the Royal Automobile Club of Victoria in a submission on behalf of its 1.3 million members to the Social Development Committee of the Victorian Parliament in 1990.Complaints have been made that speed cameras have been located a short distance before signs signalling an increase in the speed limit.

Those drivers approaching the sign who commence acceleration to reach the new limit, prior to passing the sign are caught by the camera. Placing speed cameras and similar devices at the bottom of a hill is regarded as another example of unfairness, if not entrapment.Motorists have protested that to place speed detecting devices on a highway that is clear, straight, and free of side roads is aimed more at raising of revenue than reducing the immediate danger to road users.

Although the RACV has consistently supported the use of speed cameras as a road safety initiative since their introduction in Victoria, it has acknowledged that many of its members have complained about the petty application of the cameras to what they regard as unjustified efforts at detecting minor speed infringements.

As a consequence of these complaints, the RACV investigated twenty-five speed camera locations in the state. At each place it conducted its own speed survey and investigated accident rates in the area. It concluded that eleven of the twenty-five locations had been inappropriately selected, having neither high crash rates nor excessive speeds in the vicinity. This represented over 40 per cent of the locations being surveyed. Eleven were judged to have been justifiably selected and a further four required further investigation. In the view of the RACV, the high proportion of inappropriate locations was evidence of a misuse of valuable enforcement resources.

It called for a better targeting of the cameras with the objective of placing them in locations that had poor accident records.

In this way they would be more directly aimed at driving behaviour associated with those crashes.The motoring organisation also noted that the speed cameras were being operated in a manner inconsistent with the general police policy that a visible police presence was the most effective means of deterring crime. Because the cameras were operated from cars not identified as police vehicles, they were essentially hidden and motorists were not deterred from speeding because they were unaware of any offence until an infringement notice was received some weeks after the violation. The aim of immediate deterrence was sacrificed to the hope that a more generalised deterrent effect in the future would be achieved by these covert operations.

The vehicle speed at which speed cameras were triggered for the purpose of issuing infringement notices, was originally set by police at the local speed limit plus 10 per cent with an additional 3 km/h tolerance for technical errors in the operation of the machines.The RACV argued that a more sophisticated and appropriate way of fixing the threshold would be by reference to what is known as the 85th percentile speed. This is a common measure used in speed studies. It derives a figure on what may be regarded as the safe speed for a particular location, given its environmental and traffic conditions, from the actual driving speed of the majority of drivers using that road. The figure is one at which the majority of drivers, i.e. 85 per cent, will be travelling on that road at or below it.

Only 15 per cent will be travelling above it. The 85th percentile speed may be above or below the local posted speed limit. Because the test is based on the conduct of those actually using the road, to enforce speed limits below the 85th percentile, even if drivers as a group were exceeding the local speed limit, would unfairly cause a large number of motorists to be classified as offenders. The RACV fully accepts that it is appropriate that those drivers whose speed exceeds that which is being observed by 85 per cent of all those travelling in the vicinity and which, in doing so, exceeds the lawful speed limit, should be subject to punishment.

However, in the RACV's view, most of the community hostility about the elements of unfairness and entrapment in speed cameras have arisen because infringement notices are being issued for what drivers believed to be relatively minor offences on sections of road on which motorists were adhering to the actual driving practices for that highway.Motorists object to being victimised for travelling at a speed which involved them only in attempting to drive responsibly by keeping up with the traffic flow on roadways that are safe for it.

Threats to privacy

Is the process of detecting offences through use of surreptitious photographic and other sensing devices unfair as too great an intrusion into the personal privacy of citizens? Does it lead in conjunction with the infringement notice system, to a too depersonalised form of criminal justice? Is the growth in the use of automatic detection devices and the computerised processing of offenders yet further evidence that mass surveillance of citizens has become an accepted plank of public administration in this country?

Many critics of these developments fear a diminution of the personal privacy of citizens as increasing numbers of the public become subject to some form of routine governmental surveillance in their personal lives. Whether or not there is some inherent merit in the purposes for which individual surveillance schemes were set up, the fear is that the growing use of these techniques and the likelihood of their output being linked into more complex networks for data-matching purposes, involves a dangerous political trend. It replaces trust with suspicion; presumptions of innocence with assumptions of guilt; involves large scale reversal of the ordinary onus of proof rules in criminal matters; and replaces personal responsibility with vicarious responsibility.

The risk ofcreating powerful surveillance networks by linking together data files collected for unrelated purposes has been the source of great anxiety for many.While cameras and other sensors only gather information, computers can store it indefinitely and analyse it with a speed and efficiency beyond individual human capacities. This adds a new dimension to the criminal justice system and qualitatively alters the significance of the surveillance.

The data is no longer being collected by government agencies with limited institutional memories and with systems which record information on an individual relatively inefficiently and only at a limited period of time. The knowledge and memories of organisations are now vastly extended over time and space by the new technology.

Privacy advocates argue that this is a trend to be resisted at each step of the way.Like all civil liberties issues, there are countervailing arguments. Thus, the United Kingdom North Report on the review of road traffic law, argued:United Kingdom North Report on the review of road traffic law, argued: It is sometimes implied that effective and targeted police action to detect traffic offenders by using technology is in some way unfair. We have no sympathy for the attitude which treats enforcement of the road traffic law as if it were a kind of a game, with rules that should allow the offender a sporting chance of escape. Enforcement of the road traffic law is to prevent as many as possible of the 5000 deaths and 300 000 casualties each year on the roads. That objective amply justifies the police making use of the best available means within the law to deter and detect offenders. That includes using the latest technology, and targeting the use of that technology as precisely as possible on those most likely to be in breach of the law.

There is no doubt that public anxiety about privacy considerations has been exacerbated by technical developments. Most of the early writings on the legal impact of surveillance techniques concerned the evidentiary problems which were thrown up by the use of methods which might be unlawful.But the current legal and political concerns relate to the fact that the detection and recording devices can cover larger areas, work for longer hours and with greater accuracy than ever attainable in the past by more intrusive and labour-intensive methods. It is strongly urged, in the interest of preserving civil liberties, that if policing authorities are to be given these new powers, they should be subject to even greater scrutiny and controls in the exercise of them in order to prevent manipulation or misuse of the surveillance techniques, or the databases thus created, through administrative incompetence or deliberate abuse.

Controls on Access

Many different authorities have power to issue infringement notices under Victorian legislation. However, there are both legislative restrictions on the type of infringement notice which may be issued and on access to the technology which detects offenders. For instance, local government authorities in Victoria have power to issue parking infringements, but not traffic ones. Already they have complained about their inability to control speeding within their municipal boundaries, particularly in local streets, because the police concentrate their radar beams and cameras on arterial and major roads.

So far, requests for speed cameras to be made available to municipalities, to be operated by their enforcement staff, have been denied.In 1991, with the support of the Metropolitan Municipal Association and the Municipal Association of Victoria, a number of Councils sought authority to give their by-laws officers power to issue traffic infringement notices for offences such as making illegal turns, driving through red lights and disobeying traffic signals, as well as being able to make use of speed cameras to deter excessive speed in residential areas.

The municipal authorities argued that since the government was unable to provide adequate resources for the police to monitor trafficbehaviour in local areas, there should be a devolution of enforcement power to local government to administer the Road Safety Act 1986 within local government areas.

The proposal was rejected by the police, citing the 'chaos' that would eventuate if there were local area traffic enforcement, rather than a state-wide approach. Reference was also made to the likely lack of professionalism in policing the areas, as well as the possibility that revenue raising considerations would come to predominate in the exercise of the powers being sought. The councils then adopted another tack: if they could not be trusted with the statutory powers and the equipment, could they at least purchase the equipment on condition that it was used by police locally? Early in 1992, the then municipality of Kewwrote to the Minister for Police and also to the Minister for Transport seeking to buy speed cameras to be used by local police in streets which it would nominate.

The municipality felt that an investment of $30 000 per camera would be a more efficient use of council funds than similar expenditure on installing speed humps or barriers to inhibit excessive speed in local streets. This too was rejected.A similar idea from Prahran City Council to buy a camera for local police to use in the area, provided that the revenue raised by their use of it was shared with the council, was also rejected.

This municipal government interest in acquiring speed control devices was stimulated by the government's acceptance of the 1991 recommendation of the Victorian Parliamentary Social Development Committee that speed limits for residential streets should be lowered to 50 km/h or 40 km/h near schools and shops.However, the Social Development Committee expressly considered speed cameras for local government and supported the police position that this was a specialty for them alone.This exclusion from access to speed cameras of local government authorities has been confirmed in the most recent Victorian Parliamentary Road Safety Committee Report, even though it was willing to approve of the police using civilian personnel for some of the on-road camera detection operations.

The municipalities continue to be troubledby speeding in local residential streets and motoring offences which occur near schools and other areas infrequently patrolled by police. A calculations of municipal views on metropolitan road traffic issues indicates that, after funding needs for road traffic works and services, safety and control of speed on local streets is their highest priority.

A similar resistance to police sharing access to powers and technological innovations has been evident in the United Kingdom. The intransigence of police there is a littler harder to understand since traffic wardens have been appointed for over twenty years under the Road Traffic

Regulation Act 1967 (UK) to 'discharge, in aid of the police, functions normally undertaken by the police in connection with the control and regulation of, or the enforcement of the law relating to traffic or vehicles'.

Despite their long established role in the enforcement of traffic legislation, suggestions that wardens could have a useful function in policing an infringement notice system that went beyond parking has been resisted by police, who maintain that only they have the necessary training, experience, knowledge of the law, and ability to exercise prosecutorial discretion to handle the wider range of traffic offences. Why United Kingdom traffic wardens could not obtain those skills by training similar to that provided to the police has never been satisfactorily explained.Nor have the police been immune from allegations of entrapment and revenue raising in their own use of powers which they deny to other enforcement authorities on these same grounds.

Even in the hands of police, the surveillance devices are not perfect.They are subject to error and so are their operators. One of the important ways of minimising the risk that the technology will be misused, is to ensure that technological innovations are always accompanied by legislation controlling the testing and approval of equipment, and the manner in which it may be deployed. The probity of the evidence produced by the detection devices is dependent on the performance of the device itself.

The equipment must be proved to be accurate within known and allowed for tolerances and be reliable in operation. The manufacturer's requirements in relation to the siting and calibration of devices and the training of operators and the circumstances in which the surveillance technique can properly be used, should be included in legislation or regulations. These are often adopted from standards set by the Standards Association of Australia.If police operators can betrained to reach those standards, so can others. The argument about local authorities having inadequate experience in exercising prosecutorial discretion to handle the wider range of traffic offences is hardly sustainable given the experience of municipal councils in exercising discretion in many areas of prosecutorial responsibility, and the ease with which guidelines on these matters can be prepared.

At minimum, an arrangement could be entered into whereby the infringement record could be forwarded to the Victoria Police Fixed Penalties Office or, if a photographic record, to the Traffic Camera Office for handling in accordance with the standards applicable there. The police might welcome a fee-for-service arrangement with municipalities, similar to that which many councils already have with the Melbourne City Council in the processing of infringement notices. The real objection to widening access to the new technology is that it would represent a significant expansion of social control.

Expansion of Social Control

Criminologists have been greatly interested in the manner in which social control has been expanding and how the state has shifted its involvement from direct physical punishment and restraint in custodial settings to more subtle forms of surveillance and control within the community through greater use of non-custodial sanctions.The history of infringement notices reveals how they have expanded from parking to traffic offences, and from motoring to environmental, local government, corporate and other classes of summary offending. Motoring offences still remain the major group. Even if the proportionate number of offences committed by motorists remains the same, the expanding number of motor vehicle owners in an affluent society guarantees an increase in the number of citizens under surveillance. This alone involves a marked degree of net-widening.The shift towards informalism in the disposal of summary offences has made it both easier and less expensive to extend control and surveillance by the state.

In Australia, O'Malley has already described the erosion of due process rights by the grafting of civil forms of procedure on to criminal prosecutions. This has allowed the use of lower standards of proof, the exclusion of the requirement of mens rea and the extension of responsibility for conduct beyond its immediate perpetrator. He specifically refers to the growing use of on-the-spot fines as a prime example of technocratic justice by-passing the procedures of adversary due process.

The infringement notice system combines both a judgment of guilt and the sentence in one regulatory act. It pre-empts court procedure altogether, unless challenged. However, O'Malley does not see behind these developments some kind of master plan or pattern for deliberately expanding social control and subjugating the will of the public as may be thought to exist in some totalitarian societies, but rather the results of what is seen as essentially administrative pragmatism. Foucault himself refused to seek such a 'master plan' explanation in analysing the expansion of state disciplinary power from closed institutions into the community itself. In his view, disciplinary power operates 'selffunctionally'

Another troublesome aspect of the changes brought about by the new technology is that the forms of surveillance they offer represent a change in policing style from overt to covert policing.This is more than a question of whether there are limits on the extent to which a government has a right to place its populace under surveillance. Many of these hold true for the technology already in place in support of the infringement notice system operating in Australia, or planned for the immediate future. These are:·

— The new surveillance transcends distance, darkness, and physical barriers.

— It transcends time; its records can be stored, retrieved, combined, analysed and communicated.

— It has low visibility or is invisible.

— It is often involuntary.

— Prevention is a major concern.

— It is capital, rather than labour-intensive.

— It involves decentralised self-policing.

— It triggers a shift from targeting a specific suspect to categorical suspicion of everyone.

— It is more intensive.

— It is more extensive.

These extensions in covert monitoring of citizens are occurring so gradually that it is easy to miss the magnitude of the change and the broader issues it raises. Notions of privacy, liberty, and individual rights are being shifted with little public awareness or legislative attention.Marx views the expansion of electronic forms of crime control as part of the ethos of a 'maximum security society'which spreads the discipline of the prison to society at large,and which has the following characteristics:·

— A dossier society, in which computerised records play a major role.

— An actuarial or predictive society, in which decisions are increasingly made on the basis of predictions about our future behaviour as a result of our membership in aggregate categories.

— An engineered society, in which our choices are increasingly limited and determined by the physical and social environment.

— A transparent or porous society, in which the boundaries that traditionally protected privacy are weakened.

— A self-monitored society, in which auto-surveillance plays a prominent role.

These are valid concerns. The impact of the new technology in changing the criminal justice system cannot be underestimated. The ability to inexpensively and rapidly collect, disseminate, merge and analyse data not only facilitates the expansion of social control, but adds to the citizen's sense of powerlessness and unfairness.

The fact that it is a covert and electronic process means that people do not know when and how they are being monitored and have no fair chance of controlling, or avoiding the situation. Added to the fear that there is too much surveillance by government of citizens, is the correlative concern that covert operations and automatic criminal justice allow too little surveillance of government actions by the citizens themselves, or their representatives.

The large scale removal of cases from court limits the access presently enjoyed by the public, the press, and other news media to test whether justice is being fairly administered. The checks and balances which provide the accountability of the system are being weakened. The emergence of the infringement notice system, with its technological overlay, is likely to have a far greater impact than has been realised.

The ability to detect crime from a distance, without any apparent human intervention and the capacity to exact penalties demanded by computer without the need for any face to face human contact raises a legitimate anxiety that the infringement notice system is a key building block in a dehumanised criminal justice system.

10

Digital Crime Investigation Process

In the chapter Incident Response, an "incident response methodology" is given with the following phases:

— *Pre-incident Preparation:* Prepare for an incident with proper training and infrastructure.

— *Detection of the Incident:* Identify a suspected incident.

— *Initial Response:* Verify that the incident has occurred and collect volatile evidence.

— *Response Strategy Formulation:* Determine a response based on the known facts.

— *Duplication:* Create a backup of the system.

— *Investigation:* Investigate the system to identify who, what, and how.

— *Secure Measure Implementation:* Isolate and contain the suspect system before it is rebuilt.

— *Network Monitoring:* Observe the network to monitor attacks and identify additional attacks.

— *Recovery:* Restore the system to its original state with additional security measures added.

— *Reporting:* Document the response steps and remedies taken.

— *Follow-up:* Review the response and adjust accordingly.

This methodology is oriented towards the specific scenario of responding to a critical system that is suspected of being compromised. The granularity of the phases shows the focus on verifying an attack against a live system and restoring the system to its original state. The most time consuming phase of an investigation is the analysis of the system and that is only one of the eleven phases. For the corporate incident response team this is an appropriate focus, but our needs are broader and the analysis phase must be broken into more clear phases.

Law Enforcement Process Model

The U.S. Department of Justice (DOJ) published a process model in the Electronic Crime Scene Investigation Guide. The guide is a first responder's reference to different types of electronic evidence and includes procedures that can be used to safely handle them. The guide is oriented towards those who respond to the physical crime scene, so emphasis is placed on those requirements. Little attention is paid to the analysis of the system. The following phases are given:

- — *Preparation:* Prepare equipment and tools to perform needed tasks during an investigation.
- — *Collection:* Search for and collect electronic evidence.
  - — *Secure and Evaluate the Scene:* Secure the scene to ensure the safety of people and the integrity of evidence. Potential evidence should be identified in this phase.
  - — *Document the Scene:* Document the physical attributes of the scene including photos of the computer.

  — *Evidence Collection:* Collect the physical system or make a copy of the data on the system.

— *Examination:* A technical review of the system for evidence.

— *Analysis:* The Investigation team reviews the examination results for their value in the case.

— *Reporting:* Examination notes are created after each case.

This process model is based on the standard physical crime scene investigation process model that has been well documented. As with the incident response model, this model does not give much attention to the examination and analysis process and therefore does not directly meet our design goals. This model can be confusing because it considers the collection of the physical hard disk to be the collection of electronic evidence.

At that point in the investigation, it is unknown to the investigator if the physical hard disk contains relevant electronic evidence or not. The collection of evidence typically occurs after it has been recognized, but in this model it is collected before the digital data has been examined. Therefore, the collection phase more accurately collects the physical evidence and the individual pieces of electronic evidence will be collected when it is examined.

An Abstract Process Model

Researchers at the U.S. Air Force identified the common traits that various process models had and incorporated them into an abstract process model. It has the following phases:

— *Identification:* Detect the incident or crime.

— *Preparation:* Prepare the tools, techniques, and obtain approval.

— *Approach Strategy:* Develop a strategy to maximize the collection of evidence and minimize the impact on the victim.

— *Preservation:* Isolate and secure the physical and digital evidence.

— *Collection:* Record the physical crime scene and duplicate digital evidence.

— *Examination:* Search for evidence relating to the suspected crime.

— *Analysis:* Determine significance and draw conclusions based on the evidence found. Repeat examination until a theory has been supported.

— *Presentation:* Summarize and provide an explanation of the final conclusions and theory.

— *Return Evidence:* Return the evidence that was removed from the scene back to the owner.

This process model does well at providing a general framework that can be applied to a range of incidents. In reality, the Preparation Phase should be before the Notification Phase so that the equipment and personnel are ready when the incident is detected. This model uses many of the same phases as the one given at the first Digital Forensic Research Workshop, but adds a description for each phase.

This model, and the previous DOJ model, uses the examination and analysis phases to identify and collect digital evidence. The names of these phases can be confusing because their meaning is only slightly different and it is common to have two investigators who are referring to the same tasks when they say that they are "analyzing a system" or "examining a system". The definition of examine is "to study or analyze" and the definition of analyze is "to examine methodically by separating into parts and studying their interrelations". While we agree that the two phases described in this model are different, the similarity in the names can lead to confusion.

Physical Crime Scene Investigation

For a historical perspective on investigation theory, the physical crime investigation literature was consulted. The following are the high-level phases of a crime scene investigation:

— *Crime Scene Preservation:* The first responder assists the wounded, searches for and arrests the suspect, and detains any witnesses. The scene should be secured and access restricted to authorized investigators.

— *Crime Scene Survey:* The investigator walks around the crime scene to identify obvious pieces of evidence and pieces of evidence that are transient. Initial observations of who, what, where, when, and how are documented and an initial theory is created.

— *Crime Scene Documentation:* The crime scene is documented using photographs, sketches and video. Evidence should be clearly documented and collected.

— *Crime Scene Search:* Search patterns are used to identify additional evidence that was not found in the survey. The theory developed in the survey is used to look for specific pieces of evidence that are still missing: the murder weapon for example.

— *Crime Scene Reconstruction:* The events that occurred at the crime scene are determined using the crime scene appearance, the locations and positions of the physical evidence, the forensic laboratory analysis results, and the scientific method.

This model allows the crime scene to be thoroughly documented and uses the investigator's experience to find useful pieces of evidence. Not all physical objects can be taken from the crime scene, so the Search Phase must be thorough enough to gather the needed evidence but not overload the laboratory with unrelated objects.

An Integrated Digital Investigation Process

The laws of nature bind the physical world, while the instructions in hardware and software bind the digital world. A physical crime scene investigation uses the laws of nature to find physical evidence and the digital crime scene investigation uses the code to find digital evidence.

In physical crime scene investigations, a famous theory is the Locard Exchange Principle. It states, "when two objects come into contact, a mutual exchange of matter will take place between them". For example, hairs and fibers from the criminal are frequently left behind at a physical crime scene. A similar effect can occur in a digital crime scene.

Temporary files, memory contents that are saved to disk, and deleted file fragments may exist because of a piece of software that the suspect executed. Data enters and exists the digital crime scene and leaves traces of digital evidence behind. The digital investigator is left at the mercy of the operating system and application developers though because they control what evidence is written to storage locations.

Using the concept that a computer is itself a crime scene, the investigation theory for a physical crime scene was applied to a digital investigation. The resulting process model is described in the following sections and each section includes a brief description of the actions that could be taken. The digital crime scene investigation is integrated with the physical crime scene so that physical evidence can be collected that ties the digital activity to a person. The digital crime scene can be considered a secondary crime scene to the physical crime scene.

In this field, there are many interpretations and meanings of key words. To prevent confusion, we will define the basic terms of the process. There are many definitions for each of the terms and these were chosen because they most accurately reflect our approach to the problem. Future work will include a more thorough discussion and analysis of these basic terms.

— *Physical Evidence:* Physical objects that can establish that a crime has been committed, can provide a link between a crime and its victim, or can provide a link between a crime and its perpetrator. The actual computer, hard disk, PDA, and CD-ROM are examples of physical evidence.

— *Digital Evidence:* Digital data that can establish that a crime has been committed, can provide a link between a crime and its victim, or can provide a link between a crime and its perpetrator. The data in memory, on the hard disk, or in a cell phone are examples of digital evidence.

— *Physical Crime Scene:* The physical environment where physical evidence of a crime or incident exists. The environment where the first criminal act occurred is the primary physical crime scene and subsequent scenes are secondary physical crime scenes. We created this definition based on the one given by Lee.

— *Digital Crime Scene:* The virtual environment created by software and hardware where digital evidence of a crime or incident exists. The environment where the first criminal act occurred is the primary digital crime scene and subsequent scenes are called secondary digital crime scenes.

This process model applies to both corporate and law enforcement investigations. Therefore, the terms "crime scene" and "incident" are used in the general sense. A physical crime scene is meant to include an employee's desk that is being investigated by Human Resources, a data center that contains a server that was broken into, an apartment for a child pornography investigation, or a car where a man was found murdered with his laptop open on the passenger seat. An incident is any series of events that cause a response team or evidence collection team to be deployed.

We assume that the size of a crime scene is initially defined by the natural boundaries around the known evidence. For example, if a crime is committed in a house, then the house and the property around it could be the initial physical crime scene and the size may later be increased or decreased based on the additional evidence that is found. For a computer, the initial digital crime scene is typically the virtual environment created by the local operating system and hardware. Each computer involved in an incident will likely be a separate crime scene.

The terms "examine" and "analyze" are used in this chapter to mean that an object is being processed in some way to collect information from it. As noted in the Previous Work Section, some models use these terms as separate actions, but their definitions are very similar and it can lead to confusion. The goal of this chapter is to illustrate a process model and therefore we will try to avoid confusion by only using the term "analysis", but you can replace it with examination if you prefer. The process model has 17 phases organized into five groups, which are listed here and shown in Figure 1.

1. Readiness Phases
2. Deployment Phases
3. Physical Crime Scene Investigation Phases

4. Digital Crime Scene Investigation Phases
5. Review Phase

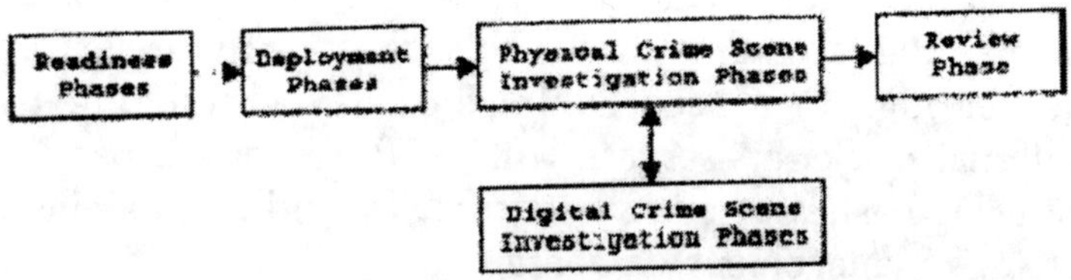

Figure 1: The five groups of phases in the investigation process.

Each phase will be discussed in the following sections. Note in the figure that the physical crime scene is processed along with the digital crime scene and the results of the digital investigation are fed into the physical crime scene investigation.

Readiness Phases

The goal of the readiness phases is to ensure that the operations and infrastructure are able to fully support an investigation. Both digital and physical evidence can be lost if it is not maintained and collected properly. This phase is ongoing and is not tied to a specific incident or crime.

The Operations Readiness Phase provides training and equipment for the personnel that will be involved with the incident and its investigation. The equipment that responders bring to the crime scene must be functioning properly and up to date. The equipment in the analysis lab should also be maintained and ready when the incident data is delivered.

The Infrastructure Readiness Phase ensures that the needed data exists for a full investigation to occur. After all, it is difficult to analyze data if it does not exist. This phase only applies to those who maintain the environment that could be the target of a crime. Physical examples for this phase include deploying video cameras and card readers to record who was in the area at the time of the crime. Digital examples for this phase include sending server logs to a secured log host, synchronizing the internal clocks on servers with NTP, creating a baseline of MD5 hashes of critical executables, and maintaining a change management database.

Deployment Phases

The goal of the deployment phases is to provide a mechanism for the incident to be detected and confirmed. The tasks performed under these phases differ widely between law enforcement and a corporate investigations team.

The Detection and Notification Phase is where an incident is detected and the appropriate people are notified. This could come in the form of a 911 call, a network-based Intrusion Detection System (IDS) alert, or an online undercover police officer who is solicited for illegal actions. This phase defines the start of the investigation process.

The Confirmation and Authorization Phase will proceed differently depending on the situation. The goal of this phase is to receive authorization to fully investigate the incident and the crime scene. For a law enforcement situation, this typically requires a search warrant or other legal approval that requires sufficient evidence or suspicion.

For corporate incidents, search warrants are not needed as long as the appropriate privacy policies are in place. In a server intrusion situation, this step typically involves the incident response team verifying that a system has been compromised by looking at the live system for evidence such as rootkits and suspicious network activity. During a live analysis to verify the incident, it is important to treat the system as a crime scene and minimize the impact to the system. After the incident has been confirmed, approval from a supervisor is typically needed to take further actions. For servers whose uptime is critical to a company, the approval may need to come from the executive level.

Physical Crime Scene Investigation Phases

The goal of the physical crime scene investigation phases is to collect and analyze the physical evidence and reconstruct the actions that took place during the incident. One of the goals of a digital investigation is to identify people who are responsible for the incident and therefore physical evidence is required. The phases presented here are the standard physical crime scene investigation phases, but this chapter focuses on the topics that are most relevant for digital incidents. For a law enforcement case, a physical crime scene expert will complete most of the tasks outlined here. In a corporate setting, they will be completed by the computer response team or the physical security team. The phases in the physical crime scene investigation phases are shown in Figure 2.

The Preservation Phase of the physical crime scene is typically indifferent to the type of crime. The activities include securing the exits, helping the wounded, detaining the suspects, and identifying witnesses. In a digital incident, the physical crime scene should be secured using the same procedures as a non-digital incident. In a server intrusion investigation, this phase may include identifying who had been in the data center and preventing others from entering because an employee could be responsible for the incident. Note that this phase preserves the crime scene so that evidence can be later identified and collected. It does not preserve specific pieces of evidence.

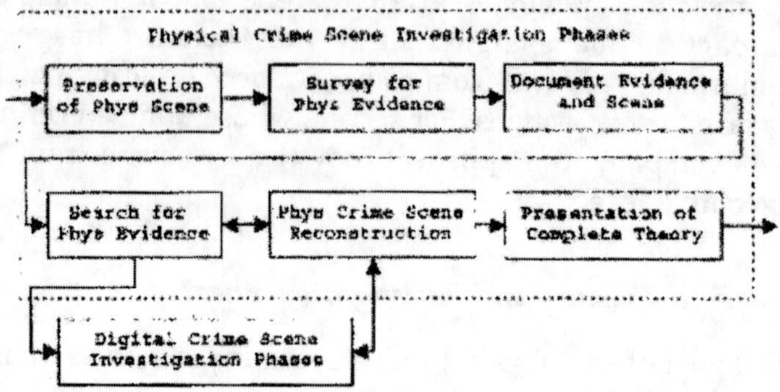

Figure 2: The six phases in the physical crime scene investigation and the interaction with the digital crime scene investigation

The Survey Phase of the physical crime scene involves a walk through of the scene by the investigator and, typically, the first person who responded to the incident. The goal is to identify the obvious pieces of physical evidence, the fragile pieces of physical evidence, and develop an initial theory about the crime. For example, in a murder investigation this phase would include walking around an apartment and identifying how the attacker gained entry, where the murder took place, and what happened to the victim after the murder. Fragile pieces of evidence should be documented and collected immediately so that they are not damaged.

In a digital incident, examples of physical evidence that are identified in the survey include the number and location of computers, what network connections the computers have, PDAs, cell phones, passwords on pieces of paper, and CD-ROMs or other removable media. At the conclusion of this phase, the investigator will have an idea about how to process the physical crime scene and what special skills are needed. If a computer specialist was not on-site at this point, one would be contacted to collect the evidence.

A computer that is running and plugged into a network can be considered fragile evidence because its digital evidence could be deleted with commands from a remote system. Therefore, some procedures include unplugging a computer from the network when it is found or deploying a network monitor to view what data is being sent to the system until the full investigation begins.

The Documentation Phase of the physical crime scene involves taking photographs, sketches, and videos of the crime scene and the physical evidence. The goal is to capture as much information as possible so that the layout and important details of the crime scene are preserved and recorded. For a digital incident, it is important to document and photograph the connections on the computer and document the state of the computer. It could also be important to document the number and size of the hard drives and the amount of memory. In some cases, the hardware MAC address of the network cards should also be recorded so that DHCP logs can used to identify the system activity. Serial numbers and asset tags are useful to record in this phase.

To identify what should be recorded, consider that the analysis lab may only get a copy of the hard disk and no original physical hardware. Anything that could be of use to the analysis lab and later reconstruction should be recorded.

The Search and Collection Phase of the physical crime scene involves an in-depth search and collection of the scene for additional physical evidence. The search can be oriented towards missing pieces of physical evidence, such as a weapon, or be methodical and have strict search patterns. Each type of evidence typically has specific procedures on how it should be collected. For a digital incident, this phase may involve looking for additional media and digital devices at the crime scene. It can also include contacting people to preserve and obtain access logs for the doors of a data center, change logs for server updates, firewall logs, IDS logs, and remote access logs. This is the last phase that typically occurs on the actual crime scene. The physical evidence that was collected from the scene is sent to labs for analysis and the results are used in the next phase, Reconstruction.

The Search and Collection Phase of the physical crime scene is where the digital crime scene investigation begins. The computer system itself will be considered physical evidence and therefore collected. The collection procedures should document how to collect volatile data from a running system and how to power it off. The digital crime scene investigation phases are outlined in detail in the next section.

The Reconstruction Phase of the physical crime scene involves organizing the analysis results from the collected physical and digital evidence and using the crime scene photographs to develop a theory for the incident. The scientific method is used with the evidence to test the incident theories. With a digital incident, the results of the digital crime scene investigation are correlated with physical evidence to link a person to the digital events.

Examples of this phase would include linking data center access logs to logins, linking on-line chat activity found on the system with the activity with an undercover officer, and linking activity on a compromised server with activity on the suspect's home system and network activity recorded by an ISP. To be most effective, this phase should involve digital crime experts to help link the events from multiple sources of digital evidence. Note that crime scene reconstruction is not the same as crime scene recreation, which makes a physical model of the crime scene.

The Presentation Phase of the physical crime scene involves presenting the physical and digital evidence to a court or corporate management. This phase presents the evidence and the theory that was developed from the physical crime scene reconstruction.

Digital Crime Scene Investigation Phases

The digital crime scene investigation phases begin when the physical digital device is collected as physical evidence from the physical crime scene or when recorded network traffic is analyzed for evidence. These phases approach the computer as a crime scene and search it for evidence. The goal is to identify the electronic events that occurred on the system and present that to the physical crime scene investigation. Someone who has specialized training with analysis tools and techniques typically performs the tasks in these phases. The phases are shown in Figure 3.

In this model, each digital device is considered a separate crime scene. The analysis results of each digital device will be sent to the Physical Crime Scene Reconstruction Phase and the linkage between the devices will be identified. This allows the analysis of different types of devices to be done at different locations. Physical crime scenes are organized into primary and secondary scenes, where the primary scene is where the first criminal act occurred. Digital crime scenes can also be organized into primary and secondary scenes. For example, the server that was broken into would be the primary digital crime scene and the log server that was later broken into to modify the logs relating to the intrusion would be a secondary digital crime scene.

The Preservation Phase of the digital crime scene involves securing the entrances and exits to the digital scene and preserving the digital evidence that could change. In the physical world, this involves reducing foot traffic and collecting physical evidence that could be lost because of weather. In the digital word, this includes isolating the system from the network, collecting the volatile data that would be lost when the system is turned off, and identifying any suspicious processes that are running on the system.

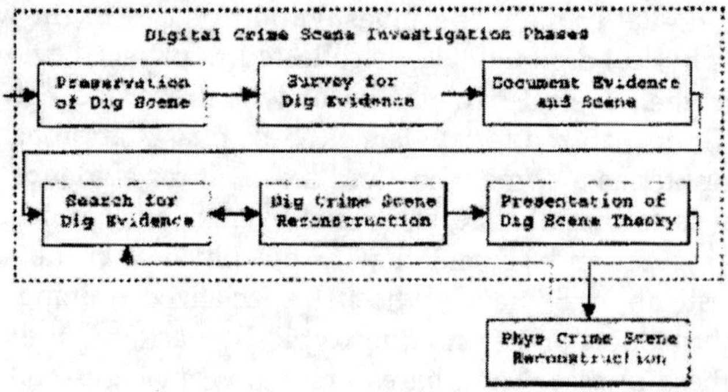

Figure 3: The six phases in the digital crime scene investigation.

Suspect users that are logged into the system should be noted and possibly investigated. Log files can be considered an eyewitness to the crime and should be secured if there is a threat that they will be lost before the system is copied. Note that other models use "preservation" to refer to preserving digital evidence. In this model, the entire digital environment is being preserved. In fact, no digital evidence has been identified yet when this phase occurs.

One of the benefits of the digital world over the physical world is that the environment can be easily replicated. Therefore, it is common in this phase to make a complete forensic image backup of the system so that it can be analyzed in a lab. This is analogous to physical investigators being able to bring an exact copy of a building into the lab for analysis.

Copies of the full disk preserve the entire digital crime scene while copies that are simply system backups preserve only the allocated data in the digital crime scene. A critical system can typically be rebuilt after a forensic image has been created so that it can be quickly placed back online. Other cases will require the original hard disk to remain as physical evidence for the duration of the case. When network monitors save network traffic, they are in effect preserving the state of the network.

The Survey Phase of the digital crime scene typically occurs in the lab using one of the digital crime scene replica images. It can occur on a live system, similar to what occurs in the physical world, but the lab environment is preferred because it provides a controlled environment and the results can be repeated with another copy of the system. If the Survey Phase is performed on a live system, then a forensic image of the system should still be taken so that any digital evidence can also be collected in a controlled lab environment. This phase is sometimes done in the field to identify if the system should be brought to the lab for a full analysis. Field searches are typically performed by booting the system into a trusted environment so that digital evidence is not modified.

The Survey Phase finds the obvious pieces of digital evidence for the given class of crime. For example, in a child pornography case the investigator would collect all of the graphic images on the system and identify those that could be used as evidence. In a server intrusion, the investigator would look for obvious signs of a rootkit installation, analyze application logs, and look for new configuration files.

Other cases may analyze the cache and history of an HTML browser. When analyzing network traffic about an incident, this phase may analyze the traffic for the incident time frame and filter out certain ports and hosts. The

Survey Phase will show the investigator the skill level of the suspect and what analysis techniques the investigation will require. The investigator may contact encryption, executable analysis, or data recovery experts at this point.

The Documentation Phase of the digital crime scene involves properly documenting the digital evidence when it is found. The exact copy of the system that was acquired during the Preservation Phase has the same role as the sketches and video of a physical crime scene. Each piece of digital evidence that is found during the analysis of the image must be clearly documented. This phase documents individual pieces of evidence and does not create the final incident say. The final output of the digital analysis will be generated in the Presentation Phase.

Digital evidence can exist in many abstraction layers and must be documented accordingly. For example, a file can be documented using its full file name path, the clusters in the file system that it uses, and the sectors on the disk that it uses. Network data can be documented with the source and target addresses at various network layers.

As digital evidence can be changed and leave little trace, additional steps should be taken to later verify the integrity. A cryptographic hash value, such as MD5 or SHA-1, should be calculated for the evidence when it is collected so that its integrity can be proven to the courts. Chain of Custody forms should be created in this phase if the evidence could be used in court. In practice, the Documentation Phase is not a specific phase in a digital investigation because the digital evidence is documented as it is found.

The Search and Collection Phase of the digital crime scene involves a thorough analysis of the system for digital evidence. This phase uses the results of the Survey Phase to focus on additional analysis types. For example, a keyword search can be performed in this phase after keywords are identified from other evidence. The unallocated file system space can be extracted and processed for deleted files.

A low-level timeline of file activity can be analyzed to trace a user's activity. Suspicious executables can be reverse engineered and encrypted files can be analyzed. All of the network packets that were collected by monitoring software can be analyzed. In some cases, it may be appropriate to examine the contents of every cluster or every file. Just as there are different search techniques in a physical crime scene, there are different techniques for a digital crime scene that can be used when appropriate.

The bulk of the investigation time is spent in this phase. In the digital world, evidence is copied from the scene and not removed from the scene. For some types of incidents, it is common to have both technical and non-technical investigators in this phase because of a limited number of trained digital investigators. For example, the technical investigator would extract all pictures from a system and send them to a non-technical investigator who would analyze each picture and identify the ones to be used as evidence. The Survey and Search Phases are similar to the Examination Phase that other models have.

The Reconstruction Phase of the digital crime scene involves putting the pieces of the digital puzzle together. The digital evidence is classified and is assessed to determine the amount of trust that can be placed in it. Data that requires advanced analysis techniques, such as executable analysis or decryption, are processed and the results are used in this phase. This phase uses the scientific method to test and reject theories based on the digital evidence.

This phase will identify how the digital evidence got there and what its existence means. When digital evidence is still missing, the Search Phase will resume to identify additional evidence. For example, in a server intrusion this phase would correlate the exploitation of a vulnerable service with the installation of a rootkit and the deployment of a network sniffer. The source IP address of network connections could lead to an additional digital crime scene to analyze. This phase is similar to the Analysis Phase that other models have.

The Presentation Phase of the digital crime scene involves presenting the digital evidence that was found to the physical crime scene investigation team. Recall that the physical crime scene team uses the results of the digital crime scene investigation in their Reconstruction Phase. Also note that the digital crime scene investigation of a system does not involve data from other digital sources, such as IDS and firewalls. The physical crime scene investigators integrate the results from each of the digital crime scenes. Therefore, this phase documents and presents the findings of a specific digital crime scene to the other investigators. In many cases, the physical and digital investigation teams are the same and the information is shared on an ongoing basis.

Review Phases

The final phase is the Review Phase and it involves reviewing the investigation to identify areas of improvement. For digital incidents, this includes how well each of the physical and digital investigations worked, how well the physical and digital investigations worked together, and whether enough physical and digital evidence existed to solve the case. The result of this phase could be new procedures, new training, or nothing if everything actually went as planned.

This model gives an accurate view of the digital investigation process and differentiates between digital evidence collection and digital forensics. Physical forensic sciences typically answer comparison questions such as "Are X and Y similar?" or identification questions such as "Can you identify X?". The actions that have historically fallen under the category of digital forensics are broader and include event reconstruction. Therefore, digital investigation is a more accurate term from the perspective of the people who are analyzing the system. From the perspective of the physical crime scene investigator who sends the computer to a lab for analysis though, the process will likely always be considered digital forensics.

This model also shows the amount of effort that needs to be dedicated to properly investigate a digital incident. Many law enforcement investigations have only one person analyzing each computer and there is a backlog of systems. This is analogous to sending one officer to a physical crime scene and expecting her to find all of the evidence and recreate the crime. Adequate resources are needed to properly investigate a digital incident.

When current technologies are examined with respect to these phases, it can be seen that the current digital "forensic" analysis tools allow the user to view the digital crime scene and collect digital evidence from it. The tools are used in the Digital Survey and Search Phases to collect evidence. Link analysis and timeline tools help the investigator in the Digital Reconstruction Phase. Therefore, with this model many current digital forensic tools may be more appropriately called digital evidence collection tools. Digital evidence collection tools translate digital data to an abstraction layer that helps the investigator. The tools use engineering techniques to display the data to the investigator and not science.

It has been debated if the evidence gathered from a live computer is reliable. Using this model, collecting evidence from a live computer is no different than collecting physical evidence. The physical crime scene will be modified when the investigator walks around just as the digital crime scene will be modified when the investigator runs digital evidence collection software. The challenge is to minimize the changes, understand the effect of the changes, and minimize the trust that is placed on the operating system of the live system.

This model clearly shows the interaction between the physical and digital realms. Many procedures focus mainly on the digital evidence and include basic physical evidence such as taking pictures of the back of the system. This model includes an equal number of phases for the physical crime scene as the digital crime scene. The motivation for this is because the end goal of any digital investigation is to tie the digital activity back to a human. Therefore, physical evidence will be needed and should be taken into account during the investigation. The digital crime scene can be considered a secondary crime scene to the physical crime scene.

The physical crime scene is well understood for law enforcement investigations. In general, the physical crime scene is less understood for digital investigations led by corporate investigators. For example, many incident response teams do not have formal procedures for analyzing the physical area around a compromised server. In reality though, a disgruntled system administrator who had physical access to the system could have performed the incident. He may have left physical evidence behind that could be lost if it is not searched for when the responders arrived.

The model also shows that the difficulties that digital investigators face are similar to those faced by physical investigators. For example, the Survey and Search Phases of both crime scenes must be able to identify the useful pieces of evidence. The physical crime investigator cannot send every physical object to the lab for analysis. He must use his experience to identify what is normal and what is not. Similarly, a digital investigator cannot send every executable on the system to be reverse engineered. Both types of investigators face the difficulty of finding small pieces of evidence, such as a hair in a carpet or a deleted file in a 100 GB file system.

Lastly, by breaking the analysis process into the Survey Phase and the Search Phase, it is easier to document and teach the process. A common problem for an inexperienced digital investigator is that he does not know how to begin the Examination Phase that other models describe. The physical investigation model of breaking the Examination Phase into two phases makes the process more intuitive. In the author's experience, digital investigations occur by finding the obvious quick hits and then expanding on them.

This chapter has outlined a process model for digital investigations that is based on the crime scene theory for physical investigations. Thousands of physical investigations have occurred and the investigation process has been refined with time. Therefore, it is useful to link a more recent type of investigation to the more established type.

This model considers the computer to be a separate crime scene and more than simply an object of physical evidence. The computer is treated more like the body at a murder scene then it is the gun. The gun will be sent for lab tests to identify if it was fired and who held it. The body is tested for chemicals in the blood stream, evidence of other abuses are searched for, and the organs are analyzed to identify how the person died, including identifying if the gun shot is what actually killed the person.

A body contains additional pieces of evidence, such as chemicals, that can be analyzed. Computers are analyzed in a manner similar to a body to identify additional pieces of evidence and the sequence of events that occurred inside of it. This model allows technical requirements for each phase to be developed and for the interaction between physical and digital investigations to be identified. It is abstract enough that it can be applied to both law enforcement and corporate scenarios. As digital evidence is challenged more in court, using procedures and models from the physical investigation world will add credibility to the analysis results from the digital world.

11

Preventing Crime

A popular urban view of rural life is that it represents an escape from much of what makes life in the cities seem so unpleasant and difficult. This includes crime. Unfortunately, as is so often the case with popular beliefs, the reality is somewhat different. Until recently, there has been little empirical evidence to document the extent of farm crime in Australia. In 2001, the Australian Institute of Criminology, funded by the Attorney General's Department, National Crime Prevention branch undertook the first of three National Farm Crime Surveys (NFCS) in Australia.

The first NFCS revealed that 27 per cent of the 1508 broadacre and dairy farms surveyed had been the victims of some form of property crime during the twelve-month survey period. The second NFCS found that 13 per cent of broadacre and dairy farms in Australia experienced some type of property crime in the previous year. The 2000-01 survey, however, measured three crime types not counted in the 2001-02 survey, namely the prevalence of dumping of rubbish on farm land, trespassing on farm land and unauthorised hunting or fishing on farm land. Excluding these three crime types reduces the prevalence rate of the 2000-01 survey to 15 per cent. The decrease in the prevalence rate between surveys is not statistically significant. The most common type of crime in the 2001-02 survey was livestock theft, experienced by six per cent of all Australian farms. The cost to the industry was estimated to be $72 million in 2001-02. In other research undertaken by Barclay et al. on farms across New South Wales it was found that more than two thirds (69 per cent) had experienced some form of property crime over the 1999-2001 period.

Importantly, 51 per cent of farmers say being a victim of two or more events of property crime, indicating a high rate of repeat victimisation. In the second NFCS, the repeat victimisation rate was found to be generally much lower, with 28 per cent of all respondents who experienced property offences say two incidents or more. Comparisons between the two surveys research must be made with caution due to the different types of farms, crimes and geographic scope in each sample. The NFCS only included farms that were classified as broadacre or dairy whereas Barclay et al sample represented a variety of farm types.

Furthermore, the crimes measured in each survey were different. Each survey measured livestock theft, other theft on the farm and vandalism and arson. However, the most recent NFCS did not include dumping of rubbish, trespassing, fraud or drug production, whereas these crimes were included in Barclay et al., research. Furthermore the NFCS was a national sample while Barclay et al., sample was drawn from New South Wales.

Comparisons with other repeat victimisation rates show that the rate of repeat victimisation on broadacre and dairy farms was higher than those recorded for break and enter and motor vehicle theft in the most recent Crime and Safety Survey and for burglary and vandalism by the Australian Institute of Criminology's Small Business Crime Survey. However, with at least one in five farmers say some level of repeat victimisation, the need for a targeted crime prevention strategy is apparent. The unique socio-demographic make up of farms can enhance opportunities for theft. Some of the factors that have been identified include:

— Remoteness and distance between properties;

— Ease of access as a result of a generally improved transport infrastructure;

— Increased population instability;

— Increasing value of livestock and other farm materials due to the drought; and

— Relaxed attitudes towards security.

Crime against farms can have a significant impact on farmers, the rural community and the farming industry as a whole. Seasonal changes such as drought can affect the type of crime perpetrated (i.e. feed/water during drought and livestock theft after the drought) and shortage of livestock and produce due to seasonal changes can have an inflationary effect on prices, thus increasing the risk of theft. This year $600 000 worth of rare livestock was stolen in a single incident in Victoria.

In addition, the latest media reports of farm crime suggest that perpetrators of crime are becoming more organised. Thieves have gone to the effort and trouble of concealing their crime by dismantling and rehanging gates, having dogs debarked, and operating by moonlight in order to avoid artificial lighting or during fog to avoid being seen. What, then, is being done or not done to help prevent crime occurring on farms?

Attitudes towards Crime Prevention

One of the key issues in developing and implementing effective crime prevention action is the attitude that the key players take towards the prevention process. If effective prevention measures are viewed as viable and achievable, it is much more likely that serious efforts will be made with regard to development and implementation.

If not, then energies and other resources are likely to be wasted on half-hearted and poorly implemented measures. None of this should be seen as surprising since, in practice, it is no more than a rational risk assessment process. As such it is not unlike the type of risk assessment that a potential offender may make when deciding whether or not to commit a particular crime in the first place.

As part of their study on the farm crime in New South Wales, Barclay et al. examined the attitudes of farmers towards security and safety on farms. The majority of farmers (60 per cent) believed that crime occurs when property owners or managers do not take sufficient responsibility for safety and security on their farm.

Furthermore, a high proportion (45 per cent) also believed that farmers should be required by law to have formal identification on farm machinery and equipment. Most importantly for crime prevention, the majority of farmers (53 per cent) believed that they had the ability to prevent crime occurring on their farm.

Furthermore, the study also identified a number of methods farmers believed could be used for effective prevention. For example, one of the key methods highlighted for the reduction and prevention of stock theft was the introduction of a National Livestock Identification Scheme (NLIS). Two-thirds of respondents believed that the NLIS would be highly beneficial in reducing livestock theft.

Current Crime Prevention Methods

Research on farm crime in New South Wales found that 64 per cent of farmers locked the farm residence when gone for the day, yet farmers were less likely to secure other areas of the farm as vigilantly. Other security methods that were commonly used by farmers were maintaining fences; storing fuel tanks out of sight and making sure that someone kept watch of the property while the owners were away. Nevertheless, a high proportion of farmers say never identifying tools, equipment or machinery (65 per cent) or farm produce (46 per cent).

Other crime prevention strategies that were rarely employed by farmers included alarm systems, no trespassing signs and security lighting. Analysis of the relationship between security measures employed on farms and victimisation found all but one had no significant effect in reducing farm crime. This may, however, be due to farmers failing to implement security measures in the first place, rather than the actual security measures themselves being ineffective.

Only one percent of farmers in the New South Wales study indicated that they did not use any form of livestock identification method, with the majority using ear tags, earmarks and branding to identify their stock. Two per cent used electronic identification. However, analysis of the relationship between the prevalence of livestock identification and stock loss from the National Farm Crime survey found that, in practice, 11 per cent of stolen livestock stolen were not identified in any form.

Issues Affecting Crime Prevention Strategies

Perhaps the most important issue constraining the implementation of effective crime prevention measures on farms is the low reporting rate of farm crime to the police. The recent NFCS found that only 50 per cent of farm crime was officially reported, a similar rate to the 2000-01 NFCS (49 per cent). The most common reason for not reporting to police was the belief that the police could do nothing about it (37 per cent). A further 17 per cent believed that the crime event was not serious enough to justify reporting.

The problem of non-reporting is compounded by the fact that when incidents are reported to police, it is often after a lengthy delay. This is one of many reasons that make the investigation of livestock theft very difficult for police.

Another reason for non-reporting, was a lack of proof of ownership by the farmer. Farm equipment and even livestock may not be adequately marked oridentified thereby making investigation and recovery evenmore difficult. Similarly, the absence of proof of ownership contributes to the thief's ability toon-sell materials or livestock stolen from farms.

The ability for victims to claim insurance is also likely to influence on the decision of whether or not to report the crime. Furthermore, victims of farm vehicle theft were the most likely to make a report to the police (82 per cent). Yet this figure is still below the average reporting rate for motor vehicle theft of 95 per cent in the general community.

Insurance against livestock theft is generally not available; therefore, farmers may see little value in reporting livestock theft. Farmers may feel that if there is little chance of recovering livestock or convicting the perpetrator, there is little reason for reporting the theft to the police. An additional impediment to reporting to police is the belief by farmers that the crime is not serious enough.

This reason was stated most commonly for theft of small tools or spare parts followed by theft of material and theft of fuel. These items were also less likely to be insured, and had less impact on the victim financially than any other crime. The limited knowledge of farming and agriculture by police has also been stated as a problem in combating farm crime. For example, if the police cannot tell the difference between certain breeds of cattle, the chance of cattle being recovered is reduced considerably. The training of specialised rural police officers in a number of jurisdictions however, is aimed at increasing police knowledge about agriculture and farming. In general, if a large proportion of farm crime is not reported to the police, the full extent of the problem is never realised. In consequence, the police may not see farm crime as a priority in their area and resources may be directed elsewhere.

In 26 per cent of cases of all livestock theft recorded in the 2001- 02 NFCS, the farmer was not sure whether the livestock was actually stolen or simply missing. This brings into question the stock management techniques that farmers employ. Most of the farmers did have some type of identification on their livestock. However, the frequency with which stock are checked and making allowances for the rate at which stock are lost to natural causes, can make it difficult to determine whether or not stock were actually stolen.

On average stock were checked once a week in the New South Wales sample. Additionally, the majority of farms attributed a loss of less than two per cent of their stock to natural causes. Lengthy intervals between checks of stock and the possibility of loss due to natural causes, may make determining whether a theft has occurred very difficult.

Police Presence

Rural police services often have to cover vast areas with limited personnel. As at 31 March 1999, 456 million hectares (59 per cent) of Australian land area was used for agricultural operations. Furthermore, farmers have noted the scant presence of police at saleyards, clearing sales or in checking transport. The majority of farmers surveyed had never or rarely seen police at saleyards (63 per cent), clearing sales (68 per cent) or during transport checks (59 per cent). In order for livestock identification and transport schemes to be effectively enforced, police presence is essential as very often stolen stock are disposed of in these ways.

Evaluation of Crime Prevention Initiatives

The Rural Watch scheme, similar to that of Neighbourhood Watch, encourages people in rural communities to report crime and suspicious activity to the police. The program is run in many locations throughout Australia as well as in the United Kingdom. The aims of the program are to reduce preventable crime, encourage reporting to police, improve relationships with police, increase knowledge sharing in the community and improve the level of farm security in rural communities. Evidence from the Scottish Farm Crime Survey found that approximately two thirds of farmers surveyed believed that Rural Watch was effective in reducing farm crime.

While there has been no formal evaluation of rural watch in Australia, general observations from New South Wales have shown that police generally thought that it was successful. However, without the full support and participation of members of the rural community, it is unlikely for the scheme to be a success. It is also difficult for farming communities to participate in the scheme due to the large distances between properties. These difficulties are compounded by the general findings that neighbourhood watch style schemes can have a high variability in their effectiveness from location to location and, as such, are often of very limited effectiveness.

Crime Stoppers are community organisations run with the assistance and support of police services, Australian Governments, the private sector and the community. The aim of these programs is to increase the reporting of rural crime. The anonymous nature of reporting was suggested as a key determinant of the programmes success, as many farmers are still reluctant to report crime for fear of retribution or being seen as a dobber. Rural crime stoppers programs encourage reporting of farm crime via television and radio advertisements, and posters and brochures.

Rural crime stoppers in Victoria began in April 2002, and has shown some success with the number of calls from rural areas increasing by 10 per cent over the past year. The effectiveness of the Western Australian rural crime stoppers program is unknown, as it has only just been implemented. In general however, the effectiveness of the rural crime stoppers programs as a crime prevention tool is not yet established.

Police Stock Squads

Police Stock squads are specialised officers with training in the investigation and prevention of stock theft. Stock squads operate in Queensland and Western Australia; rural crime investigators operate in New South Wales and rural investigators in Victoria. Research from NSW found that 82 per cent of farmers thought it was necessary to have a designated Police Stock Squad in place to control livestock theft.

The Queensland stock squad has 10 units operating in 5 police regions. The squad has been in operation since 1958 when it had 3 officers and since 1998 the squad has grown to a total of 32 officers. The squad personnel are highly trained in agricultural crime and are equipped with four-wheel drive motor vehicles, motorcycles, radios, mobile phones, cameras and lap top computers.

Access to the registrar of brands is also available via their lap top computers. A total of 32 rural crime investigators have been in place in NSW since March 2001, and may explain the slight decrease in reported thefts in 2001-02.

NSW Farm Crime Prevention Fact Sheets

As a result of the research by Barclay and colleagues, 11 farm crime prevention fact sheets were produced by The Institute for Rural Futures and the NSW Crime Prevention Division. These were aimed at disseminating information to educate New South Wales farmers about preventing crime from occurring on their farms. Some of the topics in the series include:

— Farm security

— Identification of farm machinery

— Reporting crimes to the police

— Livestock theft

— Seed and grain theft

— How to establish a neighbourhood watch or rural watch group

As yet, the effectiveness of these farm crime prevention fact sheets has not been demonstrated. Further research is needed to evaluate whether farmers in NSW are aware of the resources, whether they are used and how effective they have been in reducing victimisation on farms. In 2001 a Rural Crime Prevention program was established in eight counties in California. The crime prevention strategies fell into four categories:

Community outreach: involved educating community members about rural crime and prevention methods.

Enhanced law enforcement: High risk areas in each participating county were identified and covert operations, surveillance and stakeouts were carried out. With the use of specialised rural crime prevention units, some thieves were caught in the act.

Specialised prosecution: A vertical prosecution strategy was used by participating counties. It is thought that by using this approach, the attorney's assigned to cases gained more knowledge of farm crime, and hence developed their skills and capacities thus increasing the likelihood of prosecution.

Loss recovery efforts. The participating counties marked property for identification purposes in order to recover stolen items and reduce victimisation.

Evaluation of the Rural Crime Program found that only 1 out of 8 counties had increased rates of reporting farm crime. However, all counties that participated in the program reported better law enforcement outcomes (arrests, prosecutions and convictions) compared to the rest of the state of California.

This chapter has shown that farm crime is of serious concern in Australia. Whilst a number of initiatives are in place to prevent crime on farms, the lack of thorough evaluation makes it difficult to assess their effectiveness. In light of this, the 2002-03 National Farm Crime Survey will take a broader view of what crime prevention strategies are currently being used by farmers; whether these strategies are effective in reducing/preventing crime, and the current level of awareness of crime prevention programs/resources available to farmers.

However, on the basis of the patterns of crime revealed by recent research on rural crime in Australia it is apparent that the area most likely to have the greatest impact on reducing rural crime patterns will be a focus on repeat victimisation. Both major Australian rural crime studies have identified a high rate of repeat victimisation of between 28 per cent and 51 per cent, respectively. The high levels of repeat victimisation suggest that the crime prevention strategies currently employed are not effective. The patterns of offending also suggest a significant level of planning and organisation by a small group of repeat offenders who are probably responsible for a significant amount of the higher value losses in terms of livestock and farm equipment. However, the physical context in which much rural crime occurs suggests that many of the existing tools for targeting repeat offenders and victims will need to be carefully considered in terms of appropriateness and likely effectiveness.

Many of the principles used in reducing the incidence of repeat victimisation are likely to be highly relevant and worth considering for the following reasons:

1. Targeting repeat victimisation is an efficient means of allocating scarce resources to crime problems. Due to the limited number of police in rural areas, this may be the most efficient strategy in reducing farm crime, given the restricted resources currently in place.

2. A focus on preventing repeat victimisation is even less likely to result in displacement than unfocused crime prevention efforts. Hence, preventing repeat victimisation on farms makes it less likely that other farms will be victimised.

Coupling these principles with a well-considered collaborative prevention strategy involving police, farmers, local businesses and councils, and other key members of the community will produce a framework for action that will have the effect of overcoming the natural pessimism about the value of attempting to prevent and reduce key aspects of rural crime that were noted at the beginning of this chapter.

12

United Nations Convention against Transnational Organised Crime

Article 1

Statement of purpose

The purpose of this Convention is to promote cooperation to prevent and combat transnational organized crime more effectively.

Article 2

Use of terms

For the purposes of this Convention:

(a) "Organized criminal group" shall mean a structured group of three or more persons, existing for a period of time and acting in concert with the aim of committing one or more serious crimes or offences established in accordance with this Convention, in order to obtain, directly or indirectly, a financial or other material benefit;

(b) "Serious crime" shall mean conduct constituting an offence punishable by a maximum deprivation of liberty of at least four years or a more serious penalty;

(c) "Structured group" shall mean a group that is not randomly formed for the immediate commission of an offence and that does not need to have formally defined roles for its members, continuity of its membership or a developed structure;

(d) "Property" shall mean assets of every kind, whether corporeal or incorporeal, movable or immovable, tangible or intangible, and legal documents or instruments evidencing title to, or interest in, such assets;

(e) "Proceeds of crime" shall mean any property derived from or obtained, directly or indirectly, through the commission of an offence;

(f) "Freezing" or "seizure" shall mean temporarily prohibiting the transfer, conversion, disposition or movement of property or temporarily assuming custody or control of property on the basis of an order issued by a court or other competent authority;

(g) "Confiscation", which includes forfeiture where applicable, shall mean the permanent deprivation of property by order of a court or other competent authority;

(h) "Predicate offence" shall mean any offence as a result of which proceeds have been generated that may become the subject of an offence as defined in article 6 of this Convention;

(i) "Controlled delivery" shall mean the technique of allowing illicit or suspect consignments to pass out of, through or into the territory of one or more States, with the knowledge and under the supervision of their competent authorities, with a view to the investigation of an offence and the identification of persons involved in the commission of the offence;

(j) "Regional economic integration organization" shall mean an organization constituted by sovereign States of a given region, to which its member States have transferred competence in respect of matters governed by this Convention and which has been duly authorized, in accordance with its internal procedures, to sign, ratify, accept, approve or accede to it; references to "States Parties" under this Convention shall apply to such organizations within the limits of their competence.

Article 3

Scope of application

1. This Convention shall apply, except as otherwise stated herein, to the prevention, investigation and prosecution of:
   (a) The offences established in accordance with articles 5, 6, 8 and 23 of this Convention; and
   (b) Serious crime as defined in article 2 of this Convention; where the offence is transnational in nature and involves an organized criminal group.
2. For the purpose of paragraph 1 of this article, an offence is transnational in nature if:
   (a) It is committed in more than one State;
   (b) It is committed in one State but a substantial part of its preparation, planning, direction or control takes place in another State;
   (c) It is committed in one State but involves an organized criminal group that engages in criminal activities in more than one State; or
   (d) It is committed in one State but has substantial effects in another State.

Article 4

Protection of sovereignty

1. States Parties shall carry out their obligations under this Convention in a manner consistent with the principles of sovereign equality and territorial integrity of States and that of non-intervention in the domestic affairs of other States.

2. Nothing in this Convention entitles a State Party to undertake in the territory of another State the exercise of jurisdiction and performance of functions that are reserved exclusively for the authorities of that other State by its domestic law.

Article 5

Criminalization of participation in an organized criminal group

1. Each State Party shall adopt such legislative and other measures as may be necessary to establish as criminal offences, when committed intentionally:

   (a) Either or both of the following as criminal offences distinct from those involving the attempt or completion of the criminal activity:

      (i) Agreeing with one or more other persons to commit a serious crime for a purpose relating directly or indirectly to the obtaining of a financial or other material benefit and, where required by domestic law, involving an act undertaken by one of the participants in furtherance of the agreement or involving an organized criminal group;

      (ii) Conduct by a person who, with knowledge of either the aim and general criminal activity of an organized criminal group or its intention to commit the crimes in question, takes an active part in:

a. Criminal activities of the organized criminal group;

b. Other activities of the organized criminal group in the knowledge that his or her participation will contribute to the achievement of the above-described criminal aim;

(b) Organizing, directing, aiding, abetting, facilitating or counselling the commission of serious crime involving an organized criminal group.

2. The knowledge, intent, aim, purpose or agreement referred to in paragraph 1 of this article may be inferred from objective factual circumstances.

3. States Parties whose domestic law requires involvement of an organized criminal group for purposes of the offences established in accordance with paragraph 1 (a) (i) of this article shall ensure that their domestic law covers all serious crimes involving organized criminal groups. Such States Parties, as well as States Parties whose domestic law requires an act in furtherance of the agreement for purposes of the offences established in accordance with paragraph 1 (a) (i) of this article, shall so inform the Secretary-General of the United Nations at the time of their signature or of deposit of their instrument of ratification, acceptance or approval of or accession to this Convention.

Article 6

Criminalization of the laundering of proceeds of crime

1. Each State Party shall adopt, in accordance with

fundamental principles of its domestic law, such legislative and other measures as may be necessary to establish as criminal offences, when committed intentionally:

(a) (i) The conversion or transfer of property, knowing that such property is the proceeds of crime, for the purpose of concealing or disguising the illicit origin of the property or of helping any person who is involved in the commission of the predicate offence to evade the legal consequences of his or her action;

(ii) The concealment or disguise of the true nature, source, location, disposition, movement or ownership of or rights with respect to property, knowing that such property is the proceeds of crime;

(b) Subject to the basic concepts of its legal system:

(i) The acquisition, possession or use of property, knowing, at the time of receipt, that such property is the proceeds of crime;

(ii) Participation in, association with or conspiracy to commit, attempts to commit and aiding, abetting, facilitating and counselling the commission of any of the offences established in accordance with this article.

2. For purposes of implementing or applying paragraph 1 of this article:

(a) Each State Party shall seek to apply paragraph 1 of this article to the widest range of predicate offences;

(b) Each State Party shall include as predicate offences all serious crime as defined in article 2 of this Convention and the offences established in accordance with articles 5, 8 and 23 of this Convention. In the case of States Parties whose legislation sets out a list of specific predicate offences, they shall, at a minimum, include in such list a comprehensive range of offences associated with organized criminal groups;

(c) For the purposes of subparagraph (b), predicate offences shall include offences committed both within and outside the jurisdiction of the State Party in question. However, offences committed outside the jurisdiction of a State Party shall constitute predicate offences only when the relevant conduct is a criminal offence under the domestic law of the State where it is committed and would be a criminal offence under the domestic law of the State Party implementing or applying this article had it been committed there;

(d) Each State Party shall furnish copies of its laws that give effect to this article and of any subsequent changes to such laws or a description thereof to the Secretary-General of the United Nations;

(e) If required by fundamental principles of the domestic law of a State Party, it may be provided that the offences set forth in paragraph 1 of this article do not apply to the persons who committed the predicate offence;

(f) Knowledge, intent or purpose required as an element of an offence set forth in paragraph 1 of this article may be inferred from objective factual circumstances.

Article 7

Measures to combat money-laundering

1. Each State Party:

   (a) Shall institute a comprehensive domestic regulatory and supervisory regime for banks and non-bank financial institutions and, where appropriate, other bodies particularly susceptible to moneylaundering, within its competence, in order to deter and detect all forms of money-laundering, which regime shall emphasize requirements for customer identification, record-keeping and the reporting of suspicious transactions;

   (b) Shall, without prejudice to articles 18 and 27 of this Convention, ensure that administrative, regulatory, law enforcement and other authorities dedicated to combating money-laundering (including, where appropriate under domestic law, judicial authorities) have the ability to cooperate and exchange information at the national and international levels within the conditions prescribed by its domestic law and, to that end, shall consider the establishment of a financial intelligence unit to serve as a national centre for the collection, analysis and dissemination of information regarding potential money-laundering.

2. States Parties shall consider implementing feasible measures to detect and monitor the movement of cash and appropriate negotiable instruments across their borders, subject to safeguards to ensure proper use of information and without impeding in any way the movement of legitimate capital. Such measures may include a requirement that individuals and businesses report the cross-border transfer of substantial

quantities of cash and appropriate negotiable instruments.

3. In establishing a domestic regulatory and supervisory regime under the terms of this article, and without prejudice to any other article of this Convention, States Parties are called upon to use as a guideline the relevant initiatives of regional, interregional and multilateral organizations against money-laundering.

4. States Parties shall endeavour to develop and promote global, regional, subregional and bilateral cooperation among judicial, law enforcement and financial regulatory authorities in order to combat money laundering.

Article 8

Criminalization of corruption

1. Each State Party shall adopt such legislative and other measures as may be necessary to establish as criminal offences, when committed intentionally:

   (a) The promise, offering or giving to a public official, directly or indirectly, of an undue advantage, for the official himself or herself or another person or entity, in order that the official act or refrain from acting in the exercise of his or her official duties;

   (b) The solicitation or acceptance by a public official, directly or indirectly, of an undue advantage, for the official himself or herself or another person or entity, in order that the official act or refrain from acting in the exercise of his or her official duties.

2. Each State Party shall consider adopting such legislative and other measures as may be necessary to establish as criminal offences conduct referred to in paragraph 1 of this article involving a foreign public

official or international civil servant. Likewise, each State Party shall consider establishing as criminal offences other forms of corruption.

3. Each State Party shall also adopt such measures as may be necessary to establish as a criminal offence participation as an accomplice in an offence established in accordance with this article.

4. For the purposes of paragraph 1 of this article and article 9 of this Convention, "public official" shall mean a public official or a person who provides a public service as defined in the domestic law and as applied in the criminal law of the State Party in which the person in question performs that function.

Article 9

Measures against corruption

1. In addition to the measures set forth in article 8 of this Convention, each State Party shall, to the extent appropriate and consistent with its legal system, adopt legislative, administrative or other effective measures to promote integrity and to prevent, detect and punish the corruption of public officials.

2. Each State Party shall take measures to ensure effective action by its authorities in the prevention, detection and punishment of the corruption of public officials, including providing such authorities with adequate independence to deter the exertion of inappropriate influence on their actions.

Article 10

Liability of legal persons

1. Each State Party shall adopt such measures as may

be necessary, consistent with its legal principles, to establish the liability of legal persons for participation in serious crimes involving an organized criminal group and for the offences established in accordance with articles 5, 6, 8 and 23 of this Convention.

2. Subject to the legal principles of the State Party, the liability of legal persons may be criminal, civil or administrative.

3. Such liability shall be without prejudice to the criminal liability of the natural persons who have committed the offences.

4. Each State Party shall, in particular, ensure that legal persons held liable in accordance with this article are subject to effective, proportionate and dissuasive criminal or non-criminal sanctions, including monetary sanctions.

Article 11

Prosecution, adjudication and sanctions

1. Each State Party shall make the commission of an offence established in accordance with articles 5, 6, 8 and 23 of this Convention liable to sanctions that take into account the gravity of that offence.

2. Each State Party shall endeavour to ensure that any discretionary legal powers under its domestic law relating to the prosecution of persons for offences covered by this Convention are exercised to maximize the effectiveness of law enforcement measures in respect of those offences and with due regard to the need to deter the commission of such offences.

3. In the case of offences established in accordance with articles 5, 6, 8 and 23 of this Convention, each State Party shall take appropriate measures, in accordance

with its domestic law and with due regard to the rights of the defence, to seek to ensure that conditions imposed in connection with decisions on release pending trial or appeal take into consideration the need to ensure the presence of the defendant at subsequent criminal proceedings.

4. Each State Party shall ensure that its courts or other competent authorities bear in mind the grave nature of the offences covered by this Convention when considering the eventuality of early release or parole of persons convicted of such offences.

5. Each State Party shall, where appropriate, establish under its domestic law a long statute of limitations period in which to commence proceedings for any offence covered by this Convention and a longer period where the alleged offender has evaded the administration of justice.

6. Nothing contained in this Convention shall affect the principle that the description of the offences established in accordance with this Convention and of the applicable legal defences or other legal principles controlling the lawfulness of conduct is reserved to the domestic law of a State Party and that such offences shall be prosecuted and punished in accordance with that law.

Article 12

Confiscation and seizure

1. States Parties shall adopt, to the greatest extent possible within their domestic legal systems, such measures as may be necessary to enable confiscation of:

   (a) Proceeds of crime derived from offences covered

by this Convention or property the value of which corresponds to that of such proceeds;

(b) Property, equipment or other instrumentalities used in or destined for use in offences covered by this Convention.

2. States Parties shall adopt such measures as may be necessary to enable the identification, tracing, freezing or seizure of any item referred to in paragraph 1 of this article for the purpose of eventual confiscation.

3. If proceeds of crime have been transformed or converted, in part or in full, into other property, such property shall be liable to the measures referred to in this article instead of the proceeds.

4. If proceeds of crime have been intermingled with property acquired from legitimate sources, such property shall, without prejudice to any powers relating to freezing or seizure, be liable to confiscation up to the assessed value of the intermingled proceeds.

5. Income or other benefits derived from proceeds of crime, from property into which proceeds of crime have been transformed or converted or from property with which proceeds of crime have been intermingled shall also be liable to the measures referred to in this article, in the same manner and to the same extent as proceeds of crime.

6. For the purposes of this article and article 13 of this Convention, each State Party shall empower its courts or other competent authorities to order that bank, financial or commercial records be made available or be seized. States Parties shall not decline to act under the provisions of this paragraph on the ground of bank secrecy.

7. States Parties may consider the possibility of requiring that an offender demonstrate the lawful origin of

alleged proceeds of crime or other property liable to confiscation, to the extent that such a requirement is consistent with the principles of their domestic law and with the nature of the judicial and other proceedings.

8. The provisions of this article shall not be construed to prejudice the rights of bona fide third parties.

9. Nothing contained in this article shall affect the principle that the measures to which it refers shall be defined and implemented in accordance with and subject to the provisions of the domestic law of a State Party.

Article 13

International cooperation for purposes of confiscation

1. A State Party that has received a request from another State Party having jurisdiction over an offence covered by this Convention for confiscation of proceeds of crime, property, equipment or other instrumentalities referred to in article 12, paragraph 1, of this Convention situated in its territory shall, to the greatest extent possible within its domestic legal system:

   (a) Submit the request to its competent authorities for the purpose of obtaining an order of confiscation and, if such an order is granted, give effect to it; or

   (b) Submit to its competent authorities, with a view to giving effect to it to the extent requested, an order of confiscation issued by a court in the territory of the requesting State Party in accordance with article 12, paragraph 1, of this Convention insofar as it relates to proceeds of crime, property, equipment or other instrumentalities referred to in article 12, paragraph 1, situated in the territory of the requested State Party.

2. Following a request made by another State Party having jurisdiction over an offence covered by this Convention, the requested State Party shall take measures to identify, trace and freeze or seize proceeds of crime, property, equipment or other instrumentalities referred to in article 12, paragraph 1, of this Convention for the purpose of eventual confiscation to be ordered either by the requesting State Party or, pursuant to a request under paragraph 1 of this article, by the requested State Party.

3. The provisions of article 18 of this Convention are applicable, mutatis mutandis, to this article. In addition to the information specified in article 18, paragraph 15, requests made pursuant to this article shall contain:

   (a) In the case of a request pertaining to paragraph 1 (a) of this article, a description of the property to be confiscated and a statement of the facts relied upon by the requesting State Party sufficient to enable the requested State Party to seek the order under its domestic law;

   (b) In the case of a request pertaining to paragraph 1 (b) of this article, a legally admissible copy of an order of confiscation upon which the request is based issued by the requesting State Party, a statement of the facts and information as to the extent to which execution of the order is requested;

   (c) In the case of a request pertaining to paragraph 2 of this article, a statement of the facts relied upon by the requesting State Party and a description of the actions requested.

4. The decisions or actions provided for in paragraphs 1 and 2 of this article shall be taken by the requested State Party in accordance with and subject to the provisions of its domestic law and its procedural rules or any bilateral or multilateral treaty, agreement or arrangement to which it may be bound in relation to the requesting State Party.

5. Each State Party shall furnish copies of its laws and regulations that give effect to this article and of any subsequent changes to such laws and regulations or a description thereof to the Secretary-General of the United Nations.

6. If a State Party elects to make the taking of the measures referred to in paragraphs 1 and 2 of this article conditional on the existence of a relevant treaty, that State Party shall consider this Convention the necessary and sufficient treaty basis.

7. Cooperation under this article may be refused by a State Party if the offence to which the request relates is not an offence covered by this Convention.

8. The provisions of this article shall not be construed to prejudice the rights of bona fide third parties.

9. States Parties shall consider concluding bilateral or multilateral treaties, agreements or arrangements to enhance the effectiveness of international cooperation undertaken pursuant to this article.

Article 14

Disposal of confiscated proceeds of crime or property

1. Proceeds of crime or property confiscated by a State Party pursuant to articles 12 or 13, paragraph 1, of this Convention shall be disposed of by that State Party in accordance with its domestic law and administrative procedures.

2. When acting on the request made by another State Party in accordance with article 13 of this Convention, States Parties shall, to the extent permitted by domestic law and if so requested, give priority consideration to returning the confiscated proceeds of crime or property to the requesting State Party so that it can give compensation to the victims of the crime or return such proceeds of crime or property to their legitimate owners.

3. When acting on the request made by another State Party in accordance with articles 12 and 13 of this Convention, a State Party may give special consideration to concluding agreements or arrangements on:

   (a) Contributing the value of such proceeds of crime or property or funds derived from the sale of such proceeds of crime or property or a part thereof to the account designated in accordance with article 30, paragraph 2 (c), of this Convention and to intergovernmental bodies specializing in the fight against organized crime;

   (b) Sharing with other States Parties, on a regular or case-by-case basis, such proceeds of crime or property, or funds derived from the sale of such proceeds of crime or property, in accordance with its domestic law or administrative procedures.

Article 15

Jurisdiction

1. Each State Party shall adopt such measures as may be necessary to establish its jurisdiction over the offences established in accordance with articles 5, 6, 8 and 23 of this Convention when:

(a) The offence is committed in the territory of that State Party; or

(b) The offence is committed on board a vessel that is flying the flag of that State Party or an aircraft that is registered under the laws of that State Party at the time that the offence is committed.

2. Subject to article 4 of this Convention, a State Party may also establish its jurisdiction over any such offence when:

(a) The offence is committed against a national of that State Party;

(b) The offence is committed by a national of that State Party or a stateless person who has his or her habitual residence in its territory; or

(c) The offence is:

(i) One of those established in accordance with article 5, paragraph 1, of this Convention and is committed outside its territory with a view to the commission of a serious crime within its territory;

(ii) One of those established in accordance with article 6, paragraph 1 (b) (ii), of this Convention and is committed outside its territory with a view to the commission of an offence established in accordance with article 6, paragraph 1 (a) (i) or (ii) or (b) (i), of this Convention within its territory.

3. For the purposes of article 16, paragraph 10, of this Convention, each State Party shall adopt such measures as may be necessary to establish its jurisdiction over the offences covered by this Convention when the alleged offender is present in its territory and it does not extradite such person

solely on the ground that he or she is one of its nationals.

4. Each State Party may also adopt such measures as may be necessary to establish its jurisdiction over the offences covered by this Convention when the alleged offender is present in its territory and it does not extradite him or her.

5. If a State Party exercising its jurisdiction under paragraph 1 or 2 of this article has been notified, or has otherwise learned, that one or more other States Parties are conducting an investigation, prosecution or judicial proceeding in respect of the same conduct, the competent authorities of those States Parties shall, as appropriate, consult one another with a view to coordinating their actions.

6. Without prejudice to norms of general international law, this Convention does not exclude the exercise of any criminal jurisdiction established by a State Party in accordance with its domestic law.

Article 16

Extradition

1. This article shall apply to the offences covered by this Convention or in cases where an offence referred to in article 3, paragraph 1 (a) or (b), involves an organized criminal group and the person who is the subject of the request for extradition is located in the territory of the requested State Party, provided that the offence for which extradition is sought is punishable under the domestic law of both the requesting State Party and the requested State Party.

2. If the request for extradition includes several separate serious crimes, some of which are not covered by this

article, the requested State Party may apply this article also in respect of the latter offences.

3. Each of the offences to which this article applies shall be deemed to be included as an extraditable offence in any extradition treaty existing between States Parties. States Parties undertake to include such offences as extraditable offences in every extradition treaty to be concluded between them.

4. If a State Party that makes extradition conditional on the existence of a treaty receives a request for extradition from another State Party with which it has no extradition treaty, it may consider this Convention the legal basis for extradition in respect of any offence to which this article applies.

5. States Parties that make extradition conditional on the existence of a treaty shall:

   (a) At the time of deposit of their instrument of ratification, acceptance, approval of or accession to this Convention, inform the Secretary-General of the United Nations whether they will take this Convention as the legal basis for cooperation on extradition with other States Parties to this Convention; and

   (b) If they do not take this Convention as the legal basis for cooperation on extradition, seek, where appropriate, to conclude treaties on extradition with other States Parties to this Convention in order to implement this article.

6. States Parties that do not make extradition conditional on the existence of a treaty shall recognize offences to which this article applies as extraditable offences between themselves.

7. Extradition shall be subject to the conditions provided for by the domestic law of the requested State Party

or by applicable extradition treaties, including, inter alia, conditions in relation to the minimum penalty requirement for extradition and the grounds upon which the requested State Party may refuse extradition.

8. States Parties shall, subject to their domestic law, endeavour to expedite extradition procedures and to simplify evidentiary requirements relating thereto in respect of any offence to which this article applies.

9. Subject to the provisions of its domestic law and its extradition treaties, the requested State Party may, upon being satisfied that the circumstances so warrant and are urgent and at the request of the requesting State Party, take a person whose extradition is sought and who is present in its territory into custody or take other appropriate measures to ensure his or her presence at extradition proceedings.

10. A State Party in whose territory an alleged offender is found, if it does not extradite such person in respect of an offence to which this article applies solely on the ground that he or she is one of its nationals, shall, at the request of the State Party seeking extradition, be obliged to submit the case without undue delay to its competent authorities for the purpose of prosecution. Those authorities shall take their decision and conduct their proceedings in the same manner as in the case of any other offence of a grave nature under the domestic law of that State Party. The States Parties concerned shall cooperate with each other, in particular on procedural and evidentiary aspects, to ensure the efficiency of such prosecution.

11. Whenever a State Party is permitted under its domestic law to extradite or otherwise surrender one of its nationals only upon the condition that the person will be returned to that State Party to serve the

sentence imposed as a result of the trial or proceedings for which the extradition or surrender of the person was sought and that State Party and the State Party seeking the extradition of the person agree with this option and other terms that they may deem appropriate, such conditional extradition or surrender shall be sufficient to discharge the obligation set forth in paragraph 10 of this article.

12. If extradition, sought for purposes of enforcing a sentence, is refused because the person sought is a national of the requested State Party, the requested Party shall, if its domestic law so permits and in conformity with the requirements of such law, upon application of the requesting Party, consider the enforcement of the sentence that has been imposed under the domestic law of the requesting Party or the remainder thereof.

13. Any person regarding whom proceedings are being carried out in connection with any of the offences to which this article applies shall be guaranteed fair treatment at all stages of the proceedings, including enjoyment of all the rights and guarantees provided by the domestic law of the State Party in the territory of which that person is present.

14. Nothing in this Convention shall be interpreted as imposing an obligation to extradite if the requested State Party has substantial grounds for believing that the request has been made for the purpose of prosecuting or punishing a person on account of that person's sex, race, religion, nationality, ethnic origin or political opinions or that compliance with the request would cause prejudice to that person's position for any one of these reasons.

15. States Parties may not refuse a request for extradition on the sole ground that the offence is also considered to involve fiscal matters.

16. Before refusing extradition, the requested State Party shall, where appropriate, consult with the requesting State Party to provide it with ample opportunity to present its opinions and to provide information relevant to its allegation.
17. States Parties shall seek to conclude bilateral and multilateral agreements or arrangements to carry out or to enhance the effectiveness of extradition.

Article 17

Transfer of sentenced persons

States Parties may consider entering into bilateral or multilateral agreements or arrangements on the transfer to their territory of persons sentenced to imprisonment or other forms of deprivation of liberty for offences covered by this Convention, in order that they may complete their sentences there.

Article 18

Mutual legal assistance

1. States Parties shall afford one another the widest measure of mutual legal assistance in investigations, prosecutions and judicial proceedings in relation to the offences covered by this Convention as provided for in article 3 and shall reciprocally extend to one another similar assistance where the requesting State Party has reasonable grounds to suspect that the offence referred to in article 3, paragraph 1 (a) or (b), is transnational in nature, including that victims, witnesses, proceeds, instrumentalities or evidence of such offences are located in the requested State Party and that the offence involves an organized criminal group.

2. Mutual legal assistance shall be afforded to the fullest extent possible under relevant laws, treaties, agreements and arrangements of the requested State Party with respect to investigations, prosecutions and judicial proceedings in relation to the offences for which a legal person may be held liable in accordance with article 10 of this Convention in the requesting State Party.

3. Mutual legal assistance to be afforded in accordance with this article may be requested for any of the following purposes:

   (a) Taking evidence or statements from persons;

   (b) Effecting service of judicial documents;

   (c) Executing searches and seizures, and freezing;

   (d) Examining objects and sites;

   (e) Providing information, evidentiary items and expert evaluations;

   (f) Providing originals or certified copies of relevant documents and records, including government, bank, financial, corporate or business records;

   (g) Identifying or tracing proceeds of crime, property, instrumentalities or other things for evidentiary purposes;

   (h) Facilitating the voluntary appearance of persons in the requesting State Party;

   (i) Any other type of assistance that is not contrary to the domestic law of the requested State Party.

4. Without prejudice to domestic law, the competent authorities of a State Party may, without prior request, transmit information relating to criminal matters to a competent authority in another State Party where they believe that such information could assist the authority

in undertaking or successfully concluding inquiries and criminal proceedings or could result in a request formulated by the latter State Party pursuant to this Convention.

5. The transmission of information pursuant to paragraph 4 of this article shall be without prejudice to inquiries and criminal proceedings in the State of the competent authorities providing the information. The competent authorities receiving the information shall comply with a request that said information remain confidential, even temporarily, or with restrictions on its use. However, this shall not prevent the receiving State Party from disclosing in its proceedings information that is exculpatory to an accused person. In such a case, the receiving State Party shall notify the transmitting State Party prior to the disclosure and, if so requested, consult with the transmitting State Party. If, in an exceptional case, advance notice is not possible, the receiving State Party shall inform the transmitting State Party of the disclosure without delay.

6. The provisions of this article shall not affect the obligations under any other treaty, bilateral or multilateral, that governs or will govern, in whole or in part, mutual legal assistance.

7. Paragraphs 9 to 29 of this article shall apply to requests made pursuant to this article if the States Parties in question are not bound by a treaty of mutual legal assistance. If those States Parties are bound by such a treaty, the corresponding provisions of that treaty shall apply unless the States Parties agree to apply paragraphs 9 to 29 of this article in lieu thereof. States Parties are strongly encouraged to apply these paragraphs if they facilitate cooperation.

8. States Parties shall not decline to render mutual legal assistance pursuant to this article on the ground of bank secrecy.

9. States Parties may decline to render mutual legal assistance pursuant to this article on the ground of absence of dual criminality. However, the requested State Party may, when it deems appropriate, provide assistance, to the extent it decides at its discretion, irrespective of whether the conduct would constitute an offence under the domestic law of the requested State Party.

10. A person who is being detained or is serving a sentence in the territory of one State Party whose presence in another State Party is requested for purposes of identification, testimony or otherwise providing assistance in obtaining evidence for investigations, prosecutions or judicial proceedings in relation to offences covered by this Convention may be transferred if the following conditions are met:

    (a) The person freely gives his or her informed consent;

    (b) The competent authorities of both States Parties agree, subject to such conditions as those States Parties may deem appropriate.

11. For the purposes of paragraph 10 of this article:

    (a) The State Party to which the person is transferred shall have the authority and obligation to keep the person transferred in custody, unless otherwise requested or authorized by the State Party from which the person was transferred;

    (b) The State Party to which the person is transferred shall without delay implement its obligation to return the person to the custody of the State Party from which the person was transferred as agreed beforehand, or as otherwise agreed, by the competent authorities of both States Parties;

(c) The State Party to which the person is transferred shall not require the State Party from which the person was transferred to initiate extradition proceedings for the return of the person;

(d) The person transferred shall receive credit for service of the sentence being served in the State from which he or she was transferred for time spent in the custody of the State Party to which he or she was transferred.

12. Unless the State Party from which a person is to be transferred in accordance with paragraphs 10 and 11 of this article so agrees, that person, whatever his or her nationality, shall not be prosecuted, detained, punished or subjected to any other restriction of his or her personal liberty in the territory of the State to which that person is transferred in respect of acts, omissions or convictions prior to his or her departure from the territory of the State from which he or she was transferred.

13. Each State Party shall designate a central authority that shall have the responsibility and power to receive requests for mutual legal assistance and either to execute them or to transmit them to the competent authorities for execution. Where a State Party has a special region or territory with a separate system of mutual legal assistance, it may designate a distinct central authority that shall have the same function for that region or territory. Central authorities shall ensure the speedy and proper execution or transmission of the requests received. Where the central authority transmits the request to a competent authority for execution, it shall encourage the speedy and proper execution of the request by the competent authority.

The Secretary-General of the United Nations shall be notified of the central authority designated for this purpose at the time each State Party deposits its instrument of ratification, acceptance or approval of or accession to this Convention. Requests for mutual legal assistance and any communication related thereto shall be transmitted to the central authorities designated by the States Parties. This requirement shall be without prejudice to the right of a State Party to require that such requests and communications be addressed to it through diplomatic channels and, in urgent circumstances, where the States Parties agree, through the International Criminal Police Organization, if possible.

14. Requests shall be made in writing or, where possible, by any means capable of producing a written record, in a language acceptable to the requested State Party, under conditions allowing that State Party to establish authenticity. The Secretary-General of the United Nations shall be notified of the language or languages acceptable to each State Party at the time it deposits its instrument of ratification, acceptance or approval of or accession to this Convention. In urgent circumstances and where agreed by the States Parties, requests may be made orally, but shall be confirmed in writing forthwith.

15. A request for mutual legal assistance shall contain:

    (a) The identity of the authority making the request;

    (b) The subject matter and nature of the investigation, prosecution or judicial proceeding to which the request relates and the name and functions of the authority conducting the investigation, prosecution or judicial proceeding;

    (c) A summary of the relevant facts, except in relation to requests for the purpose of service of judicial documents;

(d) A description of the assistance sought and details of any particular procedure that the requesting State Party wishes to be followed;

(e) Where possible, the identity, location and nationality of any person concerned; and

(f) The purpose for which the evidence, information or action is sought.

16. The requested State Party may request additional information when it appears necessary for the execution of the request in accordance with its domestic law or when it can facilitate such execution.

17. A request shall be executed in accordance with the domestic law of the requested State Party and, to the extent not contrary to the domestic law of the requested State Party and where possible, in accordance with the procedures specified in the request.

18. Wherever possible and consistent with fundamental principles of domestic law, when an individual is in the territory of a State Party and has to be heard as a witness or expert by the judicial authorities of another State Party, the first State Party may, at the request of the other, permit the hearing to take place by video conference if it is not possible or desirable for the individual in question to appear in person in the territory of the requesting State Party. States Parties may agree that the hearing shall be conducted by a judicial authority of the requesting State Party and attended by a judicial authority of the requested State Party.

19. The requesting State Party shall not transmit or use information or evidence furnished by the requested State Party for investigations, prosecutions or judicial proceedings other than those stated in the request

without the prior consent of the requested State Party. Nothing in this paragraph shall prevent the requesting State Party from disclosing in its proceedings information or evidence that is exculpatory to an accused person. In the latter case, the requesting State Party shall notify the requested State Party prior to the disclosure and, if so requested, consult with the requested State Party. If, in an exceptional case, advance notice is not possible, the requesting State Party shall inform the requested State Party of the disclosure without delay.

20. The requesting State Party may require that the requested State Party keep confidential the fact and substance of the request, except to the extent necessary to execute the request. If the requested State Party cannot comply with the requirement of confidentiality, it shall promptly inform the requesting State Party.

21. Mutual legal assistance may be refused:

    (a) If the request is not made in conformity with the provisions of this article;

    (b) If the requested State Party considers that execution of the request is likely to prejudice its sovereignty, security, ordre public or other essential interests;

    (c) If the authorities of the requested State Party would be prohibited by its domestic law from carrying out the action requested with regard to any similar offence, had it been subject to investigation, prosecution or judicial proceedings under their own jurisdiction;

    (d) If it would be contrary to the legal system of the requested State Party relating to mutual legal assistance for the request to be granted.

22. States Parties may not refuse a request for mutual legal assistance on the sole ground that the offence is also considered to involve fiscal matters.

23. Reasons shall be given for any refusal of mutual legal assistance.

24. The requested State Party shall execute the request for mutual legal assistance as soon as possible and shall take as full account as possible of any deadlines suggested by the requesting State Party and for which reasons are given, preferably in the request. The requested State Party shall respond to reasonable requests by the requesting State Party on progress of its handling of the request. The requesting State Party shall promptly inform the requested State Party when the assistance sought is no longer required.

25. Mutual legal assistance may be postponed by the requested State Party on the ground that it interferes with an ongoing investigation, prosecution or judicial proceeding.

26. Before refusing a request pursuant to paragraph 21 of this article or postponing its execution pursuant to paragraph 25 of this article, the requested State Party shall consult with the requesting State Party to consider whether assistance may be granted subject to such terms and conditions as it deems necessary. If the requesting State Party accepts assistance subject to those conditions, it shall comply with the conditions.

27. Without prejudice to the application of paragraph 12 of this article, a witness, expert or other person who, at the request of the requesting State Party, consents to give evidence in a proceeding or to assist in an investigation, prosecution or judicial proceeding in the territory of the requesting State Party shall not be prosecuted, detained, punished or subjected to any

other restriction of his or her personal liberty in that territory in respect of acts, omissions or convictions prior to his or her departure from the territory of the requested State Party. Such safe conduct shall cease when the witness, expert or other person having had, for a period of fifteen consecutive days or for any period agreed upon by the States Parties from the date on which he or she has been officially informed that his or her presence is no longer required by the judicial authorities, an opportunity of leaving, has nevertheless remained voluntarily in the territory of the requesting State Party or, having left it, has returned of his or her own free will.

28. The ordinary costs of executing a request shall be borne by the requested State Party, unless otherwise agreed by the States Parties concerned. If expenses of a substantial or extraordinary nature are or will be required to fulfil the request, the States Parties shall consult to determine the terms and conditions under which the request will be executed, as well as the manner in which the costs shall be borne.

29. The requested State Party:

    (a) Shall provide to the requesting State Party copies of government records, documents or information in its possession that under its domestic law are available to the general public;

    (b) May, at its discretion, provide to the requesting State Party in whole, in part or subject to such conditions as it deems appropriate, copies of any government records, documents or information in its possession that under its domestic law are not available to the general public.

30. States Parties shall consider, as may be necessary, the possibility of concluding bilateral or multilateral agreements or arrangements that would serve the

purposes of, give practical effect to or enhance the provisions of this article.

Article 19

Joint investigations

States Parties shall consider concluding bilateral or multilateral agreements or arrangements whereby, in relation to matters that are the subject of investigations, prosecutions or judicial proceedings in one or more States, the competent authorities concerned may establish joint investigative bodies. In the absence of such agreements or arrangements, joint investigations may be undertaken by agreement on a case-by-case basis. The States Parties involved shall ensure that the sovereignty of the State Party in whose territory such investigation is to take place is fully respected.

Article 20

Special investigative techniques

1. If permitted by the basic principles of its domestic legal system, each State Party shall, within its possibilities and under the conditions prescribed by its domestic law, take the necessary measures to allow for the appropriate use of controlled delivery and, where it deems appropriate, for the use of other special investigative techniques, such as electronic or other forms of surveillance and undercover operations, by its competent authorities in its territory for the purpose of effectively combating organized crime.
2. For the purpose of investigating the offences covered by this Convention, States Parties are encouraged to conclude, when necessary, appropriate bilateral or multilateral agreements or arrangements for using

such special investigative techniques in the context of cooperation at the international level. Such agreements or arrangements shall be concluded and implemented in full compliance with the principle of sovereign equality of States and shall be carried out strictly in accordance with the terms of those agreements or arrangements.

3. In the absence of an agreement or arrangement as set forth in paragraph 2 of this article, decisions to use such special investigative techniques at the international level shall be made on a case-by-case basis and may, when necessary, take into consideration financial arrangements and understandings with respect to the exercise of jurisdiction by the States Parties concerned.

4. Decisions to use controlled delivery at the international level may, with the consent of the States Parties concerned, include methods such as intercepting and allowing the goods to continue intact or be removed or replaced in whole or in part.

Article 21

Transfer of criminal proceedings

States Parties shall consider the possibility of transferring to one another proceedings for the prosecution of an offence covered by this Convention in cases where such transfer is considered to be in the interests of the proper administration of justice, in particular in cases where several jurisdictions are involved, with a view to concentrating the prosecution.

Article 22

Establishment of criminal record

Each State Party may adopt such legislative or other

measures as may be necessary to take into consideration, under such terms as and for the purpose that it deems appropriate, any previous conviction in another State of an alleged offender for the purpose of using such information in criminal proceedings relating to an offence covered by this Convention.

Article 23

Criminalization of obstruction of justice

Each State Party shall adopt such legislative and other measures as may be necessary to establish as criminal offences, when committed intentionally:

(a) The use of physical force, threats or intimidation or the promise, offering or giving of an undue advantage to induce false testimony or to interfere in the giving of testimony or the production of evidence in a proceeding in relation to the commission of offences covered by this Convention;

(b) The use of physical force, threats or intimidation to interfere with the exercise of official duties by a justice or law enforcement official in relation to the commission of offences covered by this Convention. Nothing in this subparagraph shall prejudice the right of States Parties to have legislation that protects other categories of public officials.

Article 24

Protection of witnesses

1. Each State Party shall take appropriate measures within its means to provide effective protection from potential retaliation or intimidation for witnesses in criminal proceedings who give testimony concerning offences covered by this Convention and, as

appropriate, for their relatives and other persons close to them.

2. The measures envisaged in paragraph 1 of this article may include, inter alia, without prejudice to the rights of the defendant, including the right to due process:

   (a) Establishing procedures for the physical protection of such persons, such as, to the extent necessary and feasible, relocating them and permitting, where appropriate, non-disclosure or limitations on the disclosure of information concerning the identity and whereabouts of such persons;

   (b) Providing evidentiary rules to permit witness testimony to be given in a manner that ensures the safety of the witness, such as permitting testimony to be given through the use of communications technology such as video links or other adequate means.

3. States Parties shall consider entering into agreements or arrangements with other States for the relocation of persons referred to in paragraph 1 of this article.

4. The provisions of this article shall also apply to victims insofar as they are witnesses.

Article 25

Assistance to and protection of victims

1. Each State Party shall take appropriate measures within its means to provide assistance and protection to victims of offences covered by this Convention, in particular in cases of threat of retaliation or intimidation.

2. Each State Party shall establish appropriate procedures to provide access to compensation and restitution for victims of offences covered by this Convention.

3. Each State Party shall, subject to its domestic law, enable views and concerns of victims to be presented and considered at appropriate stages of criminal proceedings against offenders in a manner not prejudicial to the rights of the defence.

Article 26

Measures to enhance cooperation with law enforcement authorities

1. Each State Party shall take appropriate measures to encourage persons who participate or who have participated in organized criminal groups:

   (a) To supply information useful to competent authorities for investigative and evidentiary purposes on such matters as:

      (i) The identity, nature, composition, structure, location or activities of organized criminal groups;

      (ii) Links, including international links, with other organized criminal groups;

      (iii) Offences that organized criminal groups have committed or may commit;

   (b) To provide factual, concrete help to competent authorities that may contribute to depriving organized criminal groups of their resources or of the proceeds of crime.

2. Each State Party shall consider providing for the possibility, in appropriate cases, of mitigating punishment of an accused person who provides substantial cooperation in the investigation or prosecution of an offence covered by this Convention.

3. Each State Party shall consider providing for the possibility, in accordance with fundamental principles

of its domestic law, of granting immunity from prosecution to a person who provides substantial cooperation in the investigation or prosecution of an offence covered by this Convention.

4. Protection of such persons shall be as provided for in article 24 of this Convention.

5. Where a person referred to in paragraph 1 of this article located in one State Party can provide substantial cooperation to the competent authorities of another State Party, the States Parties concerned may consider entering into agreements or arrangements, in accordance with their domestic law, concerning the potential provision by the other State Party of the treatment set forth in paragraphs 2 and 3 of this article.

Article 27

Law enforcement cooperation

1. States Parties shall cooperate closely with one another, consistent with their respective domestic legal and administrative systems, to enhance the effectiveness of law enforcement action to combat the offences covered by this Convention. Each State Party shall, in particular, adopt effective measures:

   (a) To enhance and, where necessary, to establish channels of communication between their competent authorities, agencies and services in order to facilitate the secure and rapid exchange of information concerning all aspects of the offences covered by this Convention, including, if the States Parties concerned deem it appropriate, links with other criminal activities;

(b) To cooperate with other States Parties in conducting inquiries with respect to offences covered by this Convention concerning:

   (i) The identity, whereabouts and activities of persons suspected of involvement in such offences or the location of other persons concerned;

   (ii) The movement of proceeds of crime or property derived from the commission of such offences;

   (iii) The movement of property, equipment or other instrumentalities used or intended for use in the commission of such offences;

(c) To provide, when appropriate, necessary items or quantities of substances for analytical or investigative purposes;

(d) To facilitate effective coordination between their competent authorities, agencies and services and to promote the exchange of personnel and other experts, including, subject to bilateral agreements or arrangements between the States Parties concerned, the posting of liaison officers;

(e) To exchange information with other States Parties on specific means and methods used by organized criminal groups, including, where applicable, routes and conveyances and the use of false identities, altered or false documents or other means of concealing their activities;

(f) To exchange information and coordinate administrative and other measures taken as appropriate for the purpose of early identification of the offences covered by this Convention.

2. With a view to giving effect to this Convention, States Parties shall consider entering into bilateral or multilateral agreements or arrangements on direct cooperation between their law enforcement agencies and, where such agreements or arrangements already exist, amending them. In the absence of such agreements or arrangements between the States Parties concerned, the Parties may consider this Convention as the basis for mutual law enforcement cooperation in respect of the offences covered by this Convention. Whenever appropriate, States Parties shall make full use of agreements or arrangements, including international or regional organizations, to enhance the cooperation between their law enforcement agencies.

3. States Parties shall endeavour to cooperate within their means to respond to transnational organized crime committed through the use of modern technology.

Article 28

Collection, exchange and analysis of information on the nature of organized crime

1. Each State Party shall consider analysing, in consultation with the scientific and academic communities, trends in organized crime in its territory, the circumstances in which organized crime operates, as well as the professional groups and technologies involved.

2. States Parties shall consider developing and sharing analytical expertise concerning organized criminal activities with each other and through international and regional organizations. For that purpose, common definitions, standards and methodologies should be developed and applied as appropriate.

3. Each State Party shall consider monitoring its policies and actual measures to combat organized crime and making assessments of their effectiveness and efficiency.

Article 29

Training and technical assistance

1. Each State Party shall, to the extent necessary, initiate, develop or improve specific training programmes for its law enforcement personnel, including prosecutors, investigating magistrates and customs personnel, and other personnel charged with the prevention, detection and control of the offences covered by this Convention. Such programmes may include secondments and exchanges of staff. Such programmes shall deal, in particular and to the extent permitted by domestic law, with the following:

   (a) Methods used in the prevention, detection and control of the offences covered by this Convention;

   (b) Routes and techniques used by persons suspected of involvement in offences covered by this Convention, including in transit States, and appropriate countermeasures;

   (c) Monitoring of the movement of contraband;

   (d) Detection and monitoring of the movements of proceeds of crime, property, equipment or other instrumentalities and methods used for the transfer, concealment or disguise of such proceeds, property, equipment or other instrumentalities, as well as methods used in combating money laundering and other financial crimes;

   (e) Collection of evidence;

(f) Control techniques in free trade zones and free ports;

(g) Modern law enforcement equipment and techniques, including electronic surveillance, controlled deliveries and undercover operations;

(h) Methods used in combating transnational organized crime committed through the use of computers, telecommunications networks or other forms of modern technology; and

(i) Methods used in the protection of victims and witnesses.

2. States Parties shall assist one another in planning and implementing research and training programmes designed to share expertise in the areas referred to in paragraph 1 of this article and to that end shall also, when appropriate, use regional and international conferences and seminars to promote cooperation and to stimulate discussion on problems of mutual concern, including the special problems and needs of transit States.

3. States Parties shall promote training and technical assistance that will facilitate extradition and mutual legal assistance. Such training and technical assistance may include language training, secondments and exchanges between personnel in central authorities or agencies with relevant responsibilities.

4. In the case of existing bilateral and multilateral agreements or arrangements, States Parties shall strengthen, to the extent necessary, efforts to maximize operational and training activities within international and regional organizations and within other relevant bilateral and multilateral agreements or arrangements.

Article 30

Other measures: implementation of the Convention through economic development and technical assistance

1. States Parties shall take measures conducive to the optimal implementation of this Convention to the extent possible, through international cooperation, taking into account the negative effects of organized crime on society in general, in particular on sustainable development.

2. States Parties shall make concrete efforts to the extent possible and in coordination with each other, as well as with international and regional organizations:

   (a) To enhance their cooperation at various levels with developing countries, with a view to strengthening the capacity of the latter to prevent and combat transnational organized crime;

   (b) To enhance financial and material assistance to support the efforts of developing countries to fight transnational organized crime effectively and to help them implement this Convention successfully;

   (c) To provide technical assistance to developing countries and countries with economies in transition to assist them in meeting their needs for the implementation of this Convention. To that end, States Parties shall endeavour to make adequate and regular voluntary contributions to an account specifically designated for that purpose in a United Nations funding mechanism. States Parties may also give special consideration, in accordance with their domestic law and the provisions of this Convention, to contributing to the aforementioned account a percentage of the money or of the corresponding value of proceeds of crime or property confiscated in accordance with the provisions of this Convention;

(d) To encourage and persuade other States and financial institutions as appropriate to join them in efforts in accordance with this article, in particular by providing more training programmes and modern equipment to developing countries in order to assist them in achieving the objectives of this Convention.

3. To the extent possible, these measures shall be without prejudice to existing foreign assistance commitments or to other financial cooperation arrangements at the bilateral, regional or international level.

4. States Parties may conclude bilateral or multilateral agreements or arrangements on material and logistical assistance, taking into consideration the financial arrangements necessary for the means of international cooperation provided for by this Convention to be effective and for the prevention, detection and control of transnational organized crime.

Article 31

Prevention

1. States Parties shall endeavour to develop and evaluate national projects and to establish and promote best practices and policies aimed at the prevention of transnational organized crime.

2. States Parties shall endeavour, in accordance with fundamental principles of their domestic law, to reduce existing or future opportunities for organized criminal groups to participate in lawful markets with proceeds of crime, through appropriate legislative, administrative or other measures. These measures should focus on:

(a) The strengthening of cooperation between law enforcement agencies or prosecutors and relevant private entities, including industry;

(b) The promotion of the development of standards and procedures designed to safeguard the integrity of public and relevant private entities, as well as codes of conduct for relevant professions, in particular lawyers, notaries public, tax consultants and accountants;

(c) The prevention of the misuse by organized criminal groups of tender procedures conducted by public authorities and of subsidies and licences granted by public authorities for commercial activity;

(d) The prevention of the misuse of legal persons by organized criminal groups; such measures could include:

   (i) The establishment of public records on legal and natural persons involved in the establishment, management and funding of legal persons;

   (ii) The introduction of the possibility of disqualifying by court order or any appropriate means for a reasonable period of time persons convicted of offences covered by this Convention from acting as directors of legal persons incorporated within their jurisdiction;

   (iii) The establishment of national records of persons disqualified from acting as directors of legal persons; and

   (iv) The exchange of information contained in the records referred to in subparagraphs (d) (i) and (iii) of this paragraph with the competent authorities of other States Parties.

3. States Parties shall endeavour to promote the reintegration into society of persons convicted of offences covered by this Convention.

4. States Parties shall endeavour to evaluate periodically existing relevant legal instruments and administrative practices with a view to detecting their vulnerability to misuse by organized criminal groups.

5. States Parties shall endeavour to promote public awareness regarding the existence, causes and gravity of and the threat posed by transnational organized crime. Information may be disseminated where appropriate through the mass media and shall include measures to promote public participation in preventing and combating such crime.

6. Each State Party shall inform the Secretary-General of the United Nations of the name and address of the authority or authorities that can assist other States Parties in developing measures to prevent transnational organized crime.

7. States Parties shall, as appropriate, collaborate with each other and relevant international and regional organizations in promoting and developing the measures referred to in this article. This includes participation in international projects aimed at the prevention of transnational organized crime, for example by alleviating the circumstances that render socially marginalized groups vulnerable to the action of transnational organized crime.

Article 32

Conference of the Parties to the Convention

1. A Conference of the Parties to the Convention is hereby established to improve the capacity of States

Parties to combat transnational organized crime and to promote and review the implementation of this Convention.

2. The Secretary-General of the United Nations shall convene the Conference of the Parties not later than one year following the entry into force of this Convention. The Conference of the Parties shall adopt rules of procedure and rules governing the activities set forth in paragraphs 3 and 4 of this article (including rules concerning payment of expenses incurred in carrying out those activities).

3. The Conference of the Parties shall agree upon mechanisms for achieving the objectives mentioned in paragraph 1 of this article, including:

   (a) Facilitating activities by States Parties under articles 29, 30 and 31 of this Convention, including by encouraging the mobilization of voluntary contributions;

   (b) Facilitating the exchange of information among States Parties on patterns and trends in transnational organized crime and on successful practices for combating it;

   (c) Cooperating with relevant international and regional organizations and non-governmental organizations;

   (d) Reviewing periodically the implementation of this Convention;

   (e) Making recommendations to improve this Convention and its implementation.

4. For the purpose of paragraphs 3 (d) and (e) of this article, the Conference of the Parties shall acquire the necessary knowledge of the measures taken by States Parties in implementing this Convention and the

difficulties encountered by them in doing so through information provided by them and through such supplemental review mechanisms as may be established by the Conference of the Parties.

5. Each State Party shall provide the Conference of the Parties with information on its programmes, plans and practices, as well as legislative and administrative measures to implement this Convention, as required by the Conference of the Parties.

Article 33

Secretariat

1. The Secretary-General of the United Nations shall provide the necessary secretariat services to the Conference of the Parties to the Convention.

2. The secretariat shall:

   (a) Assist the Conference of the Parties in carrying out the activities set forth in article 32 of this Convention and make arrangements and provide the necessary services for the sessions of the Conference of the Parties;

   (b) Upon request, assist States Parties in providing information to the Conference of the Parties as envisaged in article 32, paragraph 5, of this Convention; and

   (c) Ensure the necessary coordination with the secretariats of relevant international and regional organizations.

Article 34

Implementation of the Convention

1. Each State Party shall take the necessary measures,

including legislative and administrative measures, in accordance with fundamental principles of its domestic law, to ensure the implementation of its obligations under this Convention.

2. The offences established in accordance with articles 5, 6, 8 and 23 of this Convention shall be established in the domestic law of each State Party independently of the transnational nature or the involvement of an organized criminal group as described in article 3, paragraph 1, of this Convention, except to the extent that article 5 of this Convention would require the involvement of an organized criminal group.

3. Each State Party may adopt more strict or severe measures than those provided for by this Convention for preventing and combating transnational organized crime.

Article 35

Settlement of disputes

1. States Parties shall endeavour to settle disputes concerning the interpretation or application of this Convention through negotiation.

2. Any dispute between two or more States Parties concerning the interpretation or application of this Convention that cannot be settled through negotiation within a reasonable time shall, at the request of one of those States Parties, be submitted to arbitration. If, six months after the date of the request for arbitration, those States Parties are unable to agree on the organization of the arbitration, any one of those States Parties may refer the dispute to the International Court of Justice by request in accordance with the Statute of the Court.

3. Each State Party may, at the time of signature, ratification, acceptance or approval of or accession to this Convention, declare that it does not consider itself bound by paragraph 2 of this article. The other States Parties shall not be bound by paragraph 2 of this article with respect to any State Party that has made such a reservation.

4. Any State Party that has made a reservation in accordance with paragraph 3 of this article may at any time withdraw that reservation by notification to the Secretary-General of the United Nations.

Article 36

Signature, ratification, acceptance, approval and accession

1. This Convention shall be open to all States for signature from 12 to 15 December 2000 in Palermo, Italy, and thereafter at United Nations Headquarters in New York until 12 December 2002.

2. This Convention shall also be open for signature by regional economic integration organizations provided that at least one member State of such organization has signed this Convention in accordance with paragraph 1 of this article.

3. This Convention is subject to ratification, acceptance or approval. Instruments of ratification, acceptance or approval shall be deposited with the Secretary-General of the United Nations. A regional economic integration organization may deposit its instrument of ratification, acceptance or approval if at least one of its member States has done likewise. In that instrument of ratification, acceptance or approval, such organization shall declare the extent of its competence with respect to the matters governed by this Convention. Such

organization shall also inform the depositary of any relevant modification in the extent of its competence.

4. This Convention is open for accession by any State or any regional economic integration organization of which at least one member State is a Party to this Convention. Instruments of accession shall be deposited with the Secretary-General of the United Nations. At the time of its accession, a regional economic integration organization shall declare the extent of its competence with respect to matters governed by this Convention. Such organization shall also inform the depositary of any relevant modification in the extent of its competence.

Article 37

Relation with protocols

1. This Convention may be supplemented by one or more protocols.
2. In order to become a Party to a protocol, a State or a regional economic integration organization must also be a Party to this Convention.
3. A State Party to this Convention is not bound by a protocol unless it becomes a Party to the protocol in accordance with the provisions thereof.
4. Any protocol to this Convention shall be interpreted together with this Convention, taking into account the purpose of that protocol.

Article 38

Entry into force

1. This Convention shall enter into force on the ninetieth day after the date of deposit of the fortieth instrument

of ratification, acceptance, approval or accession. For the purpose of this paragraph, any instrument deposited by a regional economic integration organization shall not be counted as additional to those deposited by member States of such organization.

2. For each State or regional economic integration organization ratifying, accepting, approving or acceding to this Convention after the deposit of the fortieth instrument of such action, this Convention shall enter into force on the thirtieth day after the date of deposit by such State or organization of the relevant instrument.

Article 39

Amendment

1. After the expiry of five years from the entry into force of this Convention, a State Party may propose an amendment and file it with the Secretary-General of the United Nations, who shall thereupon communicate the proposed amendment to the States Parties and to the Conference of the Parties to the Convention for the purpose of considering and deciding on the proposal. The Conference of the Parties shall make every effort to achieve consensus on each amendment. If all efforts at consensus have been exhausted and no agreement has been reached, the amendment shall, as a last resort, require for its adoption a two-thirds majority vote of the States Parties present and voting at the meeting of the Conference of the Parties.

2. Regional economic integration organizations, in matters within their competence, shall exercise their right to vote under this article with a number of votes equal to the number of their member States that are

Parties to this Convention. Such organizations shall not exercise their right to vote if their member States exercise theirs and vice versa.

3. An amendment adopted in accordance with paragraph 1 of this article is subject to ratification, acceptance or approval by States Parties.

4. An amendment adopted in accordance with paragraph 1 of this article shall enter into force in respect of a State Party ninety days after the date of the deposit with the Secretary-General of the United Nations of an instrument of ratification, acceptance or approval of such amendment.

5. When an amendment enters into force, it shall be binding on those States Parties which have expressed their consent to be bound by it. Other States Parties shall still be bound by the provisions of this Convention and any earlier amendments that they have ratified, accepted or approved.

Article 40

Denunciation

1. A State Party may denounce this Convention by written notification to the Secretary-General of the United Nations. Such denunciation shall become effective one year after the date of receipt of the notification by the Secretary-General.

2. A regional economic integration organization shall cease to be a Party to this Convention when all of its member States have denounced it.

3. Denunciation of this Convention in accordance with paragraph 1 of this article shall entail the denunciation of any protocols thereto.

Article 41

Depositary and languages

1. The Secretary-General of the United Nations is designated depositary of this Convention.

2. The original of this Convention, of which the Arabic, Chinese, English, French, Russian and Spanish texts are equally authentic, shall be deposited with the Secretary-General of the United Nations.

   In witness whereof, the undersigned plenipotentiaries, being duly authorized thereto by their respective Governments, have signed this Convention.

Index